Lessons from Rural America

*What the National Rural Center
wanted to do, did, and failed to
do—and why.*

Lessons from Rural America

JOHN N. CORNMAN
BARBARA K. KINCAID

Seven Locks Press

Publishers
Washington, D.C./Cabin John, Md.

Library of Congress Cataloging in Publication Data

Cornman, John M., 1933–
  Lessons from rural America.

  Bibliography: p.
  Includes index.
  1. National Rural Center (Washington, D.C.)—History.
  2. United States—Rural conditions. I. Kincaid,
  Barbara K., 1943–   . II. Title.
  HN85.N38C67   1984   307.7'2'06073   84-14107

ISBN 0-932020-24-0

Jacket Design by Lynn Springer
Typography and Composition by Options Type Group,
  Takoma Park, Maryland
Printed by Thomson-Shore, Inc., Dexter, Michigan

Manufactured in the United States of America

First edition, November 1984

Seven Locks Press
Publishers
P.O. Box 72
Cabin John, Md. 20818
301-320-2130

Seven Locks Press is an affiliate of Calvin Kytle Associates

To Bill, Tom, and Winifred

Foreword

RODERICK N. PETREY

The National Rural Center was in the business of helping the American people choose a future for rural people and rural places.

"Choosing a future" requires a belief that there will be a future, that it can be molded by the cumulative effect of individual and group actions taken today, that such actions can be influenced directly with good information presented persuasively to national opinion and decision makers, and that good information on which to base opinions and decisions can be discovered by hard work and intellect.

The people at the National Rural Center believed all these things. They were optimistic and hard-working with honest intellectual skills. They believed in their missions and their daily work intensely.

This book describes what they did and what they learned.

The National Rural Center was a large part of my life, both at its beginning and at its end. The beginning was in 1974. As vice president of the Edna McConnell Clark Foundation in New York City, I tried to keep in touch

Mr. Petrey was co-chairman of the National Rural Center. He is now a practicing attorney in Miami, Florida.

with events that affected the nation's poor so that I could guide the Foundation's funding decisions. A rural Southerner myself, with a strong belief that private and public funders could do much more than they were doing to help the large percentage of the nation's poor who lived in the South, I was drawn to the work of the Task Force on Southern Rural Development. That group identified and endorsed the need for a national center for the rural poor, and the Clark Foundation soon launched a series of studies to show what such a center could accomplish. An organization called the National Rural Center was born early in 1975, begun by the work of staff and consultants paid by Clark.

But the organization was an empty vessel. It had a corporate charter and paper plans and programs, but little money to put them into action. It had the support of a sterling group of national leaders (among them Ed Bishop, former chairman of the President's Commission on Rural Poverty and now president of the University of Houston; Jay Rockefeller, now governor of West Virginia; Terry Sanford, former governor of North Carolina and now president of Duke University; and Vernon Jordan, then president of the National Urban League), but it had no program staff. It had demand, but no supply.

Two men changed all that: Tom Wahman of the Rockefeller Brothers Fund in New York and Jack Cornman, a former member of the staff of the late Senator Philip A. Hart of Michigan.

Tom Wahman is one of the nation's most influential behind-the-scenes philanthropists, a quiet and persistent man of faith and vision who has worked wonders for years with little bits of the Rockefeller fortunes. Tom breathed life into the National Rural Center by finding Jack Cornman and ensuring that funds were available over a number of years, from the Estate of Winthrop Rockefeller and other funders, to keep Jack and his staff working.

viii

As president, Jack Cornman gave the Center energy, substance and integrity, and its reputation for "impeccable information." He found and encouraged the data-gatherers, analysts, and creative staff who made discoveries that were and still are important to the nation's opinion and decision makers. He also was smart enough to find Barbara Kincaid who, as the Center's director of public information, managed the Winthrop Rockefeller Awards Program for Distinguished Rural Service and contributed immeasurably to the professionalism of the Center's work. Thanks to Jack Cornman, the Center had a remarkable staff.

It also had a remarkable board. Ed Bishop and Charles Bannerman, director of Mississippi Action for Community Education (MACE), and the Delta Foundation, were chief among them. Raymond Shafer, former governor of Pennsylvania, was the guiding force behind the Rockefeller awards program. These people, and many others, invested countless hours of cheers and tears for the Center. And they are proud of every minute of their investments.

The end came in 1982. Although its influence will be felt for years to come, the Center had to close its doors; no more foundation or government grant money was available. This book is its last product. By documenting a particularly instructive experience, it presents a strong case for another National Rural Center at some future time and place.

August, 1984

Contents

Lessons from Rural America

ONE

The Setting:
Rural America

In the late 1960s and early 1970s, urban riots had
focused the attention of the public and the federal
government on problems of the poor and minorities in the
nation's larger cities. However, hidden in the hollows of
mountains, out-of-the-way towns, and declining farms, extensive poverty also persisted. In 1968, to call attention
to the plight of the rural poor, President Lyndon Johnson
appointed a national commission whose final report, *The
People Left Behind*, documents the extent of deprivation
and/or discrimination that existed throughout rural
America. Attempting to build on the work of the commission, three national foundations, the Rockefeller
Brothers Fund, the Ford Foundation, and the Edna
McConnell Clark Foundation, funded the Task Force on
Southern Rural Development, which brought together
public officials, business and labor leaders, and academic
administrators and researchers in an attempt to plot a
broad development strategy for the rural South. Even
with such efforts, however, experience made clear that
a continuing, credible presence was required at the national level to educate opinion and decision makers about
the rural setting.

In the 1970s, that setting was changing. The rural

1

population was increasing dramatically and unexpectedly (at least in the opinion of demographers), reversing population trends that had existed since before the turn of the century and encouraging the belief that a "rural renaissance" was under way. The economy was also changing, with 90 percent of the rural work force in non-farm jobs; by 1977 there were almost three times as many factory workers as farm workers in rural America. Moreover, manufacturing and service enterprises increasingly were locating in rural areas, and during the decade the growth rate of private-sector jobs in general was greater in rural areas than in urban areas.

Unfortunately, reliance on gross growth rate figures and the romanticism of "rural renaissance" rhetoric can overstate the extent of the migration and gloss over problems of rapid growth in some areas and continued decline and poverty in others. Narrowly defined concepts of rurality, inaccurately interpreted data, and ignorance of changes in the rural economy can lead to errors of omission and commission in policies designed to increase opportunities and enhance the quality of life for rural people.

First, the meaning of *rural* itself must be understood, as there is a tendency to view it as an entity, as some kind of nonmetropolitan constant. Yet those who have traveled across the land know that rural includes the Green Mountains of Vermont, a ski resort in New York, a college town in Pennsylvania, a coal mining community in Kentucky, a poor town in the Black Belt of the South, unincorporated communities of migrant farm-worker families in Texas, Indian nations in Oklahoma, family and corporate farms in the Midwest, fishing communities in Washington, and on, and on. Rural America encompasses communities of different sizes, geography, ethnicity, economic bases, rates of growth, and levels of affluence and poverty.

Second, in assessing growth rate percentages, one must remember that rural America starts from a very small base. The 1980 Census, for example, shows that there was a gain of 31.9 percent in rural population in the western states during the 1970s. This translates into slightly more than two million people. For the same ten-year period, the population of metropolitan areas of the West increased by "only" 21.2 percent, but by almost six million people. In the southern states, metropolitan areas grew at an even greater percentage than did rural areas; translating the growth rate for the southern states, eight million people moved into metropolitan areas, four million into rural areas. It is important to understand, then, that the move to the Sunbelt was to a great extent a move to metropolitan areas by both percentages and people. Otherwise, rural issues can become confused with and lost in disputes between regions. This is particularly important when considering the South, which continues to contain the majority of the nation's nine million poor rural people and most of the nation's two million poor rural blacks and Hispanics. Thus, looking behind the broad population figures and rose-tinted façade of the rural renaissance rhetoric, we find that as of 1980:

- some four hundred rural counties (out of three thousand), which tend to have an agricultural economic base or a predominantly minority population, continued to lose population;
- more than six million rural people lived in housing without adequate plumbing facilities;
- rural people were disproportionately poor, with an average annual income of $3,394 for families, $2.33 a day for each member of a family of four (although raw numbers do indicate that there were still more poor people in urban areas);

- rural black families were three times more likely to be poor than rural white families;
- predominantly black rural communities lagged behind white counties in attracting new jobs;
- poverty and unemployment rates for rural blacks were several times higher than the rates for rural whites;
- the number of farms owned by blacks continued to decline sharply, while the number of farms in general also declined; and
- the *urban* growth in the southern states resulted from a southern rural-to-urban migration as well as from the popularized Frostbelt to Sunbelt migration.*

Third, the rapid growth of rural America has also left it increasingly vulnerable to nationwide economic fluctuations. It took four years for rural areas to regain the manufacturing jobs lost during the economic downturn of 1974-75; and while the figures have yet to be compiled, early indications are that rural areas have been as hard hit as metropolitan areas during the current recession. Furthermore, in many rural areas, the rate of growth has outstripped the ability to handle demands for services and to meet expectations of new residents. This has caused conflicts between longtime residents and new migrants and has threatened the very qualities that made the communities attractive in the first place. Finally, prospects of future employment growth in rural areas is as uncertain as the impacts of past growth have been mixed. The continued decrease in the number of farms will mean increasing trouble for farm communities. The desirability of rural areas as places to live may be affected by the price and availability of energy and the ability of these communities to deliver services. Lack of public funds for

---

*For more up-to-date demographic information on the nation's rural areas, see appendix.

4

water, sewer, and other infrastructure facilities (including highways and bridges) may deter business from moving to rural communities. Thus, how conflicts over land and water use are resolved will affect potential for growth. Since 1973, service jobs have been the key factor in rural employment growth, which may signal an end to the immigration of manufacturing plants. On the other hand, advances in telecommunications and computers could make even greater diversification of economic activity possible.

In calling attention to this scattered and untidy portrait, we seek not to play down the rural renaissance, for it is a historic and unexpected turn about in migration patterns. Instead, we want to show that rural America is far more complex and diverse than is commonly perceived, and that its problems will not be solved nor its potentials attained until that diversity is understood and appropriate private and public policies are developed. Rural America is home to natural and national resources—land, water, fuels, and people—each vital to the well-being of the nation as a whole, and it is home to sixty million people, a sizable market for an economy in search of customers. Thus it would be tragic if a lack of understanding resulted in missed opportunities to increase options and enhance the quality of life for long-term rural residents, including the poor and the new immigrants.

This was the reason for the National Rural Center.

And this is the setting about which the National Rural Center sought to educate opinion and decision makers.

TWO

Why We Write,
And Some Necessary
Definitions

The National Rural Center, a private nonprofit corporation, opened for business 1 March 1976 and closed 31 August 1982. Its mission was to influence national policies affecting rural development, particularly policies benefiting the rural poor and near poor. In pursuit of its mission, the center expanded and contracted, undertook a range of projects, published, educated some decision makers, debated its purpose, and evolved into a concept and a strategy. Along the way, the center often preached that if progress were to be made, those who would "do good," presumably in the public interest, had an obligation to record their experience and advance the learning curve for those who followed.

This report is presented to meet that obligation, with the expectation that in the not-too-distant future the need for a national rural policy organization will be recognized and such an organization funded. By reporting lessons learned, we hope to help any new organization avoid the center's mistakes and build on its successes. By offering program and management recommendations, we seek, not only to suggest an effective plan of action, but also to encourage interest in and support for such an organization.

Additionally, since memory can be fanciful and/or mis-leading and all of us, including funding executives, may be subject to long but faulty memories, we write to pro-vide a record free of some of the misconceptions that often trailed the rural center experiment. For example, many potential funders remember that the center was born amid some controversy created by the announced intention of the Edna McConnell Clark Foundation to provide a $10 million grant to a new rural policy and advocacy or-ganization. Not surprisingly, more than one existing organization felt more deserving of the money than any new institution, or, failing to be the recipient, feared a grant of that size would dry up funds for other national rural organizations. For several reasons, perhaps in-cluding the controversy that greeted its announcement, the Clark Foundation never provided any direct program support to the center, although it did fund an extensive planning process that resulted in a multivolume report and developed the basis for many of the center's initia-tives. However, long after the center's founding and at odds with the facts, foundation and federal funding of-ficials continued to think of the center as the organiza-tion either funded by Clark or not funded by Clark presumably for some sound reason, although to our knowl-edge no reason was ever announced. Both misconceptions hindered fund-raising credibility. Therefore, we also write to provide a record of what the center was, what it did, and how it came to close, so that misconceptions about the center will not cloud prospects for a new rural policy organization.

The authors were the center's chief operating officer (Cornman) and its chief of information (Kincaid). Readers therefore are warned to be alert for self-serving state-ments, no matter how slight. However, readers can be comforted by the fact that neither author has any interest in being part of a second genesis of a national rural center. To that extent, at least, what follows is for the potential benefit of others.

How We Really Started

Under the preferred scenario, the center was to be launched with an endowment or operating fund of $10 million or more provided by a consortium of foundations led by the Clark Foundation. The goal was to create a stable financial base providing longevity if not permanence for a major policy analysis and advocacy organization. With the Clark decision not to provide a general operating grant, the strategy changed. Not wishing to lose the momentum and recommendations created by the planning process, the founders decided to launch a scaled-down version of the original concept and to see if it could evolve into a larger, permanent organization. This decision was supported, if not encouraged, by the Task Force on Southern Rural Development, the foundation-funded effort that brought together government, business, labor, and academic leaders from across the South to recommend policies for alleviating rural poverty in the South. The task force recommended creation of a national rural policy organization.

The center was born small with an original staff of ten persons. It was funded by a $1.5 million general operations grant from the Winthrop Rockefeller Charitable Trust (which was to be spent in four to seven years) and by $300,000 in grants from two federal agencies for specific projects. The trust grant became available as it was matched by funds from other sources.

In one respect, the decision not to provide a new organization $10 million may have been correct. The center,

8

by design, was a unique and, indeed, an experimental organization whose programs and effectiveness improved over time. Of course, with a grant of that size, the center probably would have lasted longer, and the concept of funding an experiment makes sense only if long-term support is available when the experiment proves successful. But we are less than certain that enough was known at the start to ensure the wise use of that much money. The experimental nature of the center ought to be kept in mind in evaluating what follows.

Before proceeding, however, several definitions seem in order.

Some Definitions

Few terms come laden with so much baggage as *rural, development, capacity building, data, policy,* and *process,* all terms necessary for understanding what the center was and ought to have been about.

To start with, *rural* is difficult to say clearly or at least to understand on the other end of the telephone. Often, we were referred to as the "National World Center," which says something about how people view the potential audacity of Washington-based organizations. "Rural as in country" became our automatic amplification.

Difficult as it is to say, *rural* is even harder to define. Most people equate it with farming, though by 1980 less than 10 percent of rural jobs were in farming. The federal government is not much help on definitions either, having had as many as nine major operating definitions at one time. Academicians love endlessly to debate precise definitions of such terms, ignoring the fact that such preciseness is necessary principally for the allocation of public money, which is more a political than an intellectual exercise. True, definitions are needed to organize the collection of data, but dividing the nation into just two categories (metropolitan and nonmetropolitan) can be misleading when our country is really a collection of communities stretching over a continuum from very small to very large. Further, in some regions of the country, people consider themselves residents of small towns with farmers regarded as the only rural residents. Finally, there are researchers who make their livelihood trying to discover constant traits and characteristics among rural people and rural areas, an exercise mainly useful in writing articles for professional journals and earning tenure.

The center never defined *rural* absolutely. Rather, working definitions were used in recognition of both the futility of an absolute definition and the necessity of dealing with the variances in definitions in official and unofficial use. An example of such a working definition might be communities ranging up to fifty-thousand in population, which, because they are small, tend to have limited resources for development, limited staffs for planning and implementing development programs, and no community development strategies, but tend to be much more tied to the national economy than they were before 1960. There is, of course, no magic in the fifty-thousand population figure, and, indeed, from various perspectives, the other factors in the definition are more important. Because *rural* was part of our name and figured prominently in our publications, we will continue to use the term in this report, though we are really talking about a range of different size communities and concerns that are micro rather than macro in size.

Development encompasses the many dimensions or conditions that determine the quality of life in a community: access to public services and facilities; protection or enhancement of natural environmental resources; the capacity of people and their institutions to set and attain these and related goals; and job creation and economic development.

Economic development means improving the level, distribution, and stability of earnings and employment and creating diverse, resilient local economies. These can be achieved by increasing productivity or efficiency of existing firms and by expanding economic activity through enlargement of existing firms and attraction of new enterprises. It is important to understand in communities where growth is rapid, perhaps too rapid, that the desired economic development trend might be a reduction in the growth rate.

Capacity is the ability of local organizations and communities to plan and carry out development strategies and projects. *Capacity-building* programs provide data and information that can improve the chances for successful implementation of development strategies and programs. The definition obviously covers a broad range of services and assistance, which includes helping a small town maintain financial records, collecting data to justify a development project proposal, designing and/or reviewing the plans for a proposed water and sewer system, providing information for advocacy efforts, etc.

Data includes all the information needed on which to base an adequate national rural policy. Too little is known about the extent of poverty, unemployment, and underemployment in rural areas; about who is moving where for what reasons; about the impact of fewer farms on the quality of life in rural communities; about the costs of delivering services in rural areas; about the quality of education in rural schools, etc. There is need to identify data gaps and improve current data collection efforts in rural areas. New data collection efforts should include pro-

11

gram documentation and evaluation as well as the gathering of statistics.

A *policy* consists of goals, action programs, and a process for bringing action programs to bear on achieving goals. In rural development policy, for example, the goal could be increased economic opportunities and improved quality of life for rural residents. An action program could include investment strategies of private firms, federal housing or water and sewer grants and loan programs, or state highway building projects. *Process* could include any of a number of different kinds of capacity-building programs. In this report, *policy* refers to the policies of the public and private sectors and includes program regulations, executive pronouncements, and agency actions, as well as legislation and actions voted by boards of directors, trustees, etc.

Policy research involves the primary collection and analysis of new data and the translation of findings into policy recommendations. "Policy analysis is the systematic examination of existing data and the application of logic and reasoning in choosing the best policy among a number of possible alternatives."*

The *policy-making process* refers to the way policies are designed, enacted, and implemented. The process consists, or at least ought to consist, of these steps: identification of problems and/or goals; definition of issues, causes, and options; creation of attention and support; selection of options by executives; adoption of options (as recommended or amended) by authorizing body (board of directors, legislature); writing of administrative procedures and program regulations to implement policy; implementation; and evaluation and recommendations for reform.

---

* Chester W. Douglass, "Definition of Health Policy Research and Policy Analysis," *Journal of Dental Education,* 44(1980): 517-19.

12

The process also consists of formal and informal parts. The former includes selection and ratification of options, writing of regulations, implementation, and evaluation. The latter is where issues are first identified and given shape, and where potential options are generated. It is here that decision makers have the necessary opportunity to learn about an issue, think the unthinkable, and explore the widest possible range of options. Such activity is ill-suited for public forums, if for no other reason than that such deliberations may prove embarrassing, misleading, and/or self-defeating. While it is true that no decision maker can long afford to appear publicly as vacillating or indecisive, it is also true that when recommendations are rushed prematurely into the formal part of the process, positions can harden before they are fully explored. Equally important, those who seek to influence policy must come in at the informal part or be limited to making changes at the margins of decisions already made, which is where many public-interest advocacy groups operate. There is nothing inherently wrong with the existence of the informal part of the policy-making process from a rural development perspective other than the fact that rural issues are too seldom addressed there. That conclusion and some ideas on how to correct that problem might be the most important lessons learned from our experience.

THREE

What the Center Tried To Be, More or Less

B ecause the center was created to influence national development policies benefiting the rural poor and near poor, much of its attention focused on the South, where 80 percent of the rural poor live. The center, however, took a broad, national approach to its mission because of the following assumptions:

1. Data can influence if not generate policy by showing the need for action, providing information for policy design, rationalizing a decision already made, and helping sell recommendations or positions. But to do this, the right piece of paper has to land on the right desk at the right time. Despite the existence of various advocacy groups with a rural interest and of some rural policy research and analysis activity around the country, in the 1970s few such papers on rural development issues were reaching the desks of key decision makers in Washington.

2. A narrowly drawn development policy devised and implemented in isolation from other development issues and from community-level realities can be ineffective or even counterproductive, particularly in rural areas lacking financial resources and person-

nel to provide necessary supportive activities. Also, just the availability of single-purpose programs can encourage adoption of inappropriate or wasteful strategies. Should a community concentrate on seeking a federally supported doctor for whom it might be relatively easy to obtain funds, or should it seek to clean up a polluted water supply? Will a producers' cooperative help small-farm operators if farmers don't have a market for their products? Which comes first: an industrial park or the tenants for it? Will availability of venture capital or small business technical assistance alone attract successful enterprises, or are both required at the same time? Such questions and relationships suggest how important it is to understand connections between various development efforts and the extent to which these efforts are successful in different communities. The connections are dynamic and not always predictable. Availability of health care can enhance the growth and employability of individuals, create jobs, attract commerce, and make a community attractive to businesses in search of new locations. The creation of jobs can provide an economic base to support group health insurance plans and medical facilities, and improve the physical and mental health of unemployed and underemployed persons. It can also cause health problems through pollution.

3. Public policy recommendations (even those accompanied by compelling data) without the support of a large and/or well-funded constituency tend to remain recommendations. Strategies dealing with only one rural region, with one rural issue, or with rural poverty alone reduce an already small and diffuse constituency to the point of ineffectiveness. Civil rights legislation did not result from the efforts of blacks

15

or of Southerners alone. There won't be a federal small-farms policy until people outside of small-farm families become interested in the issue. The fate of a health delivery program serving rural people may depend more on a senator from Montana who serves on the right committee than on poverty groups lobbying a southern senator opposed to development programs in general, and the senator from Montana may be more likely to take an interest if the policy serves his rural constituents as well as rural residents of the South.

Based on these assumptions, the center adopted a strategy which sought to

- create a political milieu receptive to rural development policies by educating decision and opinion makers and the broader public to the potentials and problems of rural areas;

- encourage design and implementation of development policies that would be effective and efficient both in increasing economic opportunities and in enhancing the quality of life in rural areas, particularly for the rural poor and near poor; and

- encourage creation of broader, more effective constituencies for rural development policies and programs.*

The strategy was to be cumulative in that it sought to amass an ever-increasing rural development information base and expertise. In addition, policy recommendations would help create rural networks, which would help educate policy makers and the general public, who would seek

---

* A statement of goals and objectives approved by the center's board of directors in 1979 appears in the appendixes.

and support new policy recommendations, which networks would use to educate, and so on.

Clearly, the strategy was beyond the reach of any single organization. The center's role was to be the catalyst that would link the worlds of advocacy, policy makers, and the general public by providing sound and timely information and policy recommendations to all three, and letting others take the public lead in promoting recommendations when they would, the center taking the lead when necessary.

To carry out its mission, the center engaged in policy research and analysis, demonstration projects, information collection and dissemination, networking, and advocacy. The center was organized in three components: programs, information, and administration. The first consisted of program areas in data and capacity building,* economic development, education, health and nutrition, and human services, with additions in energy and transportation under constant discussion. The second component included newsletters and other publications, an awards program recognizing leaders in rural development, and the center's rural development information service. The third included office and fiscal management, planning, and fund-raising.

Since the purpose of this report is to recommend for the future rather than to justify the past, we concede that the center's ambitious mission was not achieved. How close did the center come? That judgment would be better left to others.

Before we turn to the center's activities and to the lessons learned, however, it might help to summarize the organizational concept that evolved along the way.

---

* This program area was concerned with federal data collection efforts and technical assistance programs, and with providing general date analysis for the center.

17

The center attempted to blend two nonprofit sector traditions—advocacy and research, a difficult role given that neither rests comfortably with the other. Research organizations tend to be cautious when it comes to policy, advocacy types can be impetuous, and both tend to deal with fragments rather than entire problems.

Why then attempt the blend? For two reasons: credibility and politics.

Credibility with policy makers requires thoughtful, well-documented recommendations as the basis for policy positions. With rural people—people wary of endless, overly cautious research without conclusions—credibility requires advocacy.

Also, the blend of research and advocacy appeared to be the only concept that could work in the political milieu of the nation and rural areas. Rural people by attitude and voting records are "conservative." The issues of poverty and development are often perceived as "liberal," particularly if the public sector is to be involved. The labels of conservative and liberal, though popular in the media and politics, are roadblocks to understanding issues and barriers to consensus and change. To move beyond those labels, it was necessary to develop and sell sound recommendations that focused on real problems and opportunities.

The blend then sought to challenge the ivory tower research community to deal with realities and relevant research, the concerns of activism, and the nature and politics of change, and to stretch beyond the comfortable boundaries of narrow disciplines. It sought to challenge the ideologues of advocacy to avoid shrill and poorly documented claims, to develop recommendations from the best available research, and to look beyond the comfortable boundaries of single-issue advocacy to an expanded constituency committed to change. And it sought to challenge both not only to look beyond fragments of issues to the whole but also to offer concrete, useful, and timely recommendations.

The plan was to pull the best from each tradition, turn it into a comfortable forum for public policy consideration, work it, add some local experience and expertise at dissemination, and the result would be programmatic rural policy—progress. Or so we thought and still think it could be.

The blend? Schizophrenic and heretical, confounding convention. Different and at odds with purists from both traditions, the blend was hard to sell. It remains, nevertheless, the most effective concept for the political milieu of the nation and rural areas.

FOUR

What the Center Did—in Part

In the six and a half years of its existence, the center raised and spent about $10 million; employed as many as fifty people at one time; published or had published seventy-five reports, four newsletters, and a book; testified before Congress three or four times a year; held more than ten major conferences; and confused a lot of people about its mission and strategy.

The confusion resulted from 1) the evolving, experimental nature of the effort, 2) the tendency of observers to view the program from their own narrow perspectives, 3) a program driven too much by restricted grants (about 80 percent of its funds were awarded for specific projects), 4) the diffuse character of rural issues, and 5) the diversity of its staff.

While it was not always apparent to outside observers, there was a unifying theme to the center's approach: collecting, translating, and disseminating sound information to policy makers on rural development issues. But that theme was blurred for the following reasons:

- Potential users of the center's information were not used to an organization concerned about a range of issues as opposed to one (housing, rural health, preservation of car mufflers).

• Community-based groups did not find all the information useful and tended to discount the value of information not meant to serve the practitioner.

• Policy makers, often those who had not provided funds to support timely analysis of issues, sometimes received information too late for their immediate needs.

• Academics often did not appreciate the importance of timing in providing policy makers information and often were suspicious of information collected at the grass roots that did not fit preconceived theories.

• The center pursued too long a fund-raising strategy based on individual grants rather than on support for an overall, well-defined program. The former approach, while successful in raising money, made it impossible to pursue as well-defined a program as might have been desired. The latter approach, which would have allowed the center to offer just such a program, in the end did not attract the funding.

• And finally, while the center preached an interrelated, comprehensive, approach to rural development, its program was organized around single-topic areas (education, health, economic development, etc.), a hangover from the way the center was initially formed. The center might have been multidisciplinary; it never became interdisciplinary.

Even with the confusion, the center did carry out a number of ongoing programs as well as projects. The complete list of its publications appears in the appendix and gives some indication of the breadth and depth of the operation. This section will just provide examples of the different approaches used to carry out the center's mission.

In assessing the center's activities and impacts one must remember that its mission was to work with and through other organizations, which often made it difficult to document results. One should also recall that the center sought to be a synergistic organization, in which the various activities were to relate to and build on each other. The program was not meant to be a series of individual, fragmented projects that concluded with final reports, as is the case with many for-profit consulting firms; rather, it was hoped that what was learned one year would be the basis for more effective action the next year. Clearly, with many activities determined by project grants, that goal was not always achieved, but the center was successful on enough occasions, in our view, to support the validity of the concept. The examples that follow were selected to demonstrate that contention. As noted previously, the center engaged in policy research, policy analysis, demonstration projects, networking, information dissemination, and public education. The activities reported here were chosen also as examples of those functions.

Research and demonstration project

For most of its existence, the center was involved in activities related to or stemming from efforts to increase the benefits that minority and/or poor people would receive from construction of the Tennessee-Tombigbee Waterway through some of the poorest black counties in Mississippi and Alabama. The center's project was launched, at least conceptually, by Dr. Ray Marshall, a leading rural development economist who had been staff director of the Task Force on Southern Rural Development, then the first president of the center, and eventually secretary of labor under President Jimmy Carter.

The Ten-Tom Waterway, as it has become known, was to be one of the largest projects ever built by the U.S. Corps of Engineers. Dr. Marshall, through a study of Tennessee Valley Authority construction programs, found that rural people living in the area of the construction were not recruited and hired as construction workers on the projects. Based on that study, Dr. Marshall and others designed a strategy to adapt an employment outreach model, which had worked in urban places, to a rural setting. The model involved community-based organizations, contractors, labor unions, federal agencies, and affirmative action plans to recruit, train, and hire minority and/ or poor persons living in the general area of a project as construction workers. To broaden the test of the model's utility in rural areas, the approach was to be pursued simultaneously at five other publicly funded construction projects in the rural South.

The center had both an operational and a research role: to participate in the demonstration as the neutral catalyst that would convene the various and often antagonistic actors required to make the model work; and to collect and analyze data, to document impacts, and to make policy recommendations for future efforts. To carry out this ambitious undertaking, it was decided, partly by design and partly by accident, to staff field offices in Atlanta, Georgia, and in Austin, Texas, which, partly by accident and partly by design, grew into regional offices, which, partly by accident and partly by design, attempted to take on lives of their own, all of which created funding and administrative problems and intra-organizational tensions.

The dual role of the center also created tensions, with the researchers often unhappy with the quality of data collected by the operational staff and the operational staff bothered by having to collect data in the first place. Also, staff never resolved the "and/or" problem: was the model to serve primarily minorities and/or poor people regardless of race? Further, the center's effort was funded jointly by the U.S. Labor Department's Office of Research and Office of National Programs, both of which had different goals and reasons for providing support. And finally, many of the "public interest" advocacy groups with which the center worked in Washington considered the Ten-Tom Waterway a boondoggle that ought not be built. Although these groups claimed allegiance to the cause of grass-roots involvement in development policies, they never accepted the view of the minority and poverty organizations on the scene that construction of the waterway was the only chance these counties had of attracting significant amounts of federal development dollars. Even more disquieting, many in this advocacy contingent never appeared to comprehend the disparity between their rhetoric and practice.

However, even with these problems, the effort to establish a rural employment outreach model did produce some useful results. Moreover, it was beginning to evolve into a broader approach to rural economic development when Ronald Reagan won the White House and, as do most new presidents taking over from the other party, automatically discarded all initiatives started under Jimmy Carter. In noting these results, one should remember that a number of organizations were involved and were instrumental in achieving the outcomes. These organizations included the Federation of Southern Cooperatives, the Minorities People's Council of the Tennessee-Tombigbee Waterway, several local and national unions, area contractors, and, however reluctantly, the U.S. Corps of Engineers. These results included

- imposition of the first affirmative action hiring plan on a large rural construction project;
- increases in minority participation in training programs and the work force from negligible to 85 percent

of the new slots in apprentice programs and to 30 percent of 2100 construction jobs;
- involvement of rural citizen-based organizations in employment training and economic development programs;
- a Corps of Engineers office more sensitive to previously ignored equal employment opportunities responsibilities;
- a demonstration that the employment outreach model could work in rural areas; and
- a three-part final report of research findings, policy recommendations, and instructions for rural groups wishing to establish employment outreach programs.

One of the hooks used to gain the cooperation of the Corps of Engineers was something called "area development benefits." These benefits are gains in employment and economic growth, which are supposed to accrue to the area because of the construction projects. The value of these projected benefits are crucial to building the positive benefit-cost ratio required for a project to receive congressional approval. The ratio for the Ten-Tom Waterway was close to the minimal acceptable figure. For that reason, the corps had a strong interest in increasing the number of local persons hired to build the waterway in order to meet projected area development benefits.

While the center's initial effort focused principally on employment, it also became clear that the expected economic development benefits would not occur without special effort. One reason, at least, was fairly simple. Area economic development concerns were seldom considered by corps, state, or local planners. The center found, for example, that the corps selected for recreational areas land along the waterway that also was most appropriate for industrial or business sites, but the latter use never figured in the selection process. Further, while the corps was required to purchase some supplies and equipment from small businesses, those in the area were seldom notified in advance about what materials were to be purchased. Local small businesses with small inventories did not have appropriate supplies in stock and were not informed in time to change their inventories. As a result, the business went out of the community.

Based on these findings and on the center's reports on the rural employment outreach model, the Carter administration developed a rural initiative designed to encourage economic development in the areas of five major construction projects around the country. The center prepared eight background papers for the planning process and was monitoring the progress of these initiatives when Mr. Reagan's election ended the effort.

Despite the untimely cessation of this activity, we suggest the experience demonstrates the utility of an ongoing program that can build on past experience and evolve into a more effective source of expertise.

Policy analysis

Despite the large number of poor people living in rural areas and the fact that the states with the largest rural poor populations tend to have the lowest level of public assistance benefits, welfare reforms have seldom focused on the plight of the rural poor. To call public attention to these facts and to suggest reforms that could assist the majority of the rural poor, the center, using existing data, published a report in 1978 documenting who the rural poor were and where they lived, comparing public assistance programs in rural and nonrural states, analyzing what changes in federal public assistance programs would mean to the rural poor and to the states with large rural populations, and recommending policy changes.

The report, entitled *The Rural Stake in Public Assistance*, despite its length and difficult format, became a widely used reference document, in part because it filled a pressing need for information, and in part because it was the only data source of its kind. The center distributed more than four thousand copies, some free but most for a minimal charge. The report was used

- to influence the design of President Carter's major welfare reform proposal;
- to attract the support of national organizations for the administration's bill;
- to secure attention in the national press;
- by local groups in four Southern states to lobby successfully ten Southern congressmen to vote for the bill;
- as a basis for analyzing the impacts of proposed changes in health and child care legislation on the rural poor;
- as a resource by a task force of the National Academy of Science on rural data needs; and
- as documentation for proposals prepared by numerous nonprofit organizations.

In one sense, the many uses of the report proved the effectiveness of the right piece of paper being at the right place at the right time, for the information contained within affected the design of legislation and helped secure the votes needed to pass a bill in the U.S. House of Representatives. However, the experience also demonstrated the limits of sound information, for the bill died when President Carter chose not to fight for it in the Senate. Welfare reform (as opposed to welfare cuts) is difficult enough to enact with the support of a president; it is impossible to enact without such support.

Perhaps even more discouraging, *The Rural Stake in*

Public Assistance remained the basic source of data longer than it should have. While the center did finally print an abbreviated update in 1982, no similar comprehensive report identifying current trends in rural poverty has been produced. The need for such data and the need to keep the issue of rural poverty on the national agenda prove the contention, at least to us, of the need for an organization that would produce such information on a regular and continuing basis.

Networking

In the center's strategy, networking was a method both for disseminating the results of policy research and policy analysis and for building constituencies to work for change at the national level. The center used a number of different mechanisms, including newsletters, special mailings, conferences, and telephone pyramids. Rather than assign responsibility for networking activities to a single person or office, it asked each program area to develop its own network of policy makers, practitioners, and researchers. It was also the center's intention, for example, to try to bring together persons interested in rural development, rural health care, and the environment around an issue in which each group has a stake, such as safe drinking water. The reasoning behind the dream was, of course, the understanding that separately most rural constituencies are too small to be effective; together, they might be large enough to be heeded. Unhappily, the center never found time—or resources—to pursue that lofty goal.

Not surprisingly, the quantity and quality of networking varied greatly, depending on the skill and interest of individual program directors. Further, the center was not successful in meshing the various networks, despite its allegiance to interdisciplinary, comprehensive approaches to rural issues. However, the center was successful enough with at least one single-topic network to demonstrate the usefulness of networking. That was the rural health network, organized around concerns of delivering health care in medically underserved rural areas. The network grew out of the Southern Rural Health Care Conference, which the center helped organize in 1976, and it was developed through a four-times-a-year newsletter, close monitoring of key issues, and special mailings and telephone calls. The network was instrumental in

- increasing federal appropriations for several rural health programs;
- securing passage of a change in law to allow Medicare fees to be paid to nurse practitioners in medically underserved rural areas; and
- designing appropriate regulations to implement the change in the Medicare law.

The last effort is particularly instructive. The regulations to implement the change in Medicare to allow payments to nurse practitioners were being written by civil servants in Baltimore who had little or no firsthand experience with rural communities. Drawing on their experience with operations far larger than most rural clinics, the civil servants came up with regulations more suitable to urban settings. Through its network, the center was able to bring the practical problems that the regulations would create to the attention of the regulation writers, who did respond by changing what they had written. After two unsuccessful tries, the civil servants asked the center to set up a series of conferences around the country at which they could meet and discuss the program face-to-face with people most affected by the proposed regulations. That is a model that ought to be repeated for all drafters of program regulations, urban, suburban, or rural! In addition, the center's health staff also convened an informal network of Washington-based groups interested in rural health policies. This effort was useful in monitoring federal activities as well as bringing the influence of additional groups to bear on particular issues.

In retrospect, if the center had had more time or had been more skillful, it might well have put together a most impressive broad base rural development constituency, consisting of persons who had received its newsletters; participated in conferences, projects, and networks; requested information; and purchased a center publication. That list totaled more than twenty thousand persons.

Information dissemination

As noted previously, networks were a mechanism for disseminating information, but the information services of the center extended beyond networking. From its inception, the center was designed to be a source of information about rural issues, whether the information was developed through its own projects or came from secondary sources. Each employee, including the president and individual program directors, was expected to respond to requests for information in his or her area of expertise. Backing up the program staff was a rural development library and library staff of the highest professional quality. The library provided an excellent information base for the center's activities as well as an accessible data source for persons interested in rural development issues and programs. The collection had 400 reference volumes; 450 periodicals; more than 5,000 catalogued books, monographs, technical reports, and unpublished documents; and more than 1900 congressional and federal executive branch reports. A computer terminal linked the staff with more than a hundred other data bases. Services included interlibrary loan, borrowing privileges, legislative tracking, telephone reference, and literature searches. In addition, rural people and researchers for several years had access to the library and the center's staff through a toll-free 800 telephone number.

Users ranged from small-town mayors to federal bureaucrats, from community activists to corporate officials, from individual researchers in the field to the Library of Congress. In 1981, the center estimated it made more than one hundred thousand information contacts through newsletters, publications, speeches, letters, and telephone calls, not counting multiple readers of single copies of written materials. Frank A. Fratoe of the Economic Development Division, U.S. Department of Agriculture, praised the library as being "probably the most comprehensive, compact, and readily accessible source of rural development literature in the Washington area."

In addition to the library staff, credit for development of this resource should go to several far-seeing civil servants in the Economic Development Administration (EDA) who approved start-up and continuing support grants for several years. EDA also supported publication of the Rural Information Bibliographic Service, affectionately known to the staff as RIBS. Approximately ten times a year, RIBS reported on the latest acquisitions to the library's collection. These included all EDA publications on rural issues, which helped the agency publicize the availability of the material. Even with its limited circulation, RIBS was much in demand. One unexpected benefit was readers calling attention to publications or sending in unpublished material they thought should be in the center's collection.

There are many reasons to lament the closing of the center (it paid our salaries, for one), but by far the most lamentable is the loss of this expanding resource to the Washington scene and rural people generally.

The collection was donated to Tuskegee Institute in Alabama, where, given adequate funding support, it can be developed as a regional information data base. However, given the budgetary restraints being felt by all colleges and universities, such support, no doubt, will have to come from outside the institute. For the record, our proceeds from the sale of this book go to the rural development library at Tuskegee.

Public education

Obviously, every activity in which the center engaged, with the exception of management, could be considered public education. However, there were activities pursued by the center that do not fit easily into the other functional categories. These were its roles as a publisher and a convener.

Judging by the demand for its publications, which ran as high as five hundred a month in its last year of operation, the center was meeting some informational need. The range of topics was broad: for example, the state-of-art book on European balanced growth policies; the first resource guide to arts as an instigator of development in rural places; primers on development finance; directories of rural organizations and of resources for rural development projects; an analysis of barriers to economically self-sufficient medical practices in rural areas; a series of monographs on issues affecting the financial viability of small farms; recommendations for a small-farms research program; an evaluation of equal employment programs in the rural South; data on small rural schools; and a study of federal youth programs in rural areas.

It is, of course, more difficult to assess the center's effectiveness as a convener, but the center spent considerable time acting in this capacity. Over the years, it developed the ability to bring together representatives of groups that should have been conferring on rural issues but were not. For example, the many different federal agencies involved in some aspect of rural development issues lacked a mechanism for interagency exchange of information and views on rural programs. The center, as a nongovernmental entity that worked with many of the agencies, hosted periodic meetings of their representatives, which featured special speakers or discussions of currently "hot" issues. In the latter case, the center's staff might have prepared background papers.

Because of turf and style problems (their turf and our style), the center was less successful as a convener of Washington-based advocacy organizations, though even here the center had some successes in bringing the worlds of government and advocacy together.

However, small research conferences, which brought together researchers, policy makers, and practitioners in activities being studied, perhaps were the center's most innovative and useful public education mechanism. Conference participants were selected carefully to represent experience and geographic diversity. The conferences, usually thirty to fifty persons in size, included a mix of small discussion sessions, in which the emphasis was on securing the views of participants, and a limited number of plenary sessions, used primarily to set the background for and to share the results of the discussion groups. Staff or outside experts prepared background material and potential policy options, which the conferees were free to accept, modify, reject, or ignore.

Actually, that this methodology might be considered innovative came as a surprise, for it seemed the logical approach to joining the worlds of academia, policy making, and practice. As a matter of fact, it didn't occur to the staff that it was using a formalized approach until a rural group in Arkansas asked if "the methodology" were written down. It wasn't, so the center sent a staff person to help the group plan a statewide program planning effort.

No doubt "innovative" is a bit too self-congratulatory, for we are certain the approach had been used before and often, but we must admit that our cursory review of the rural development field, at least, found no similar attempts to bring researchers, policy makers, and practitioners face-to-face to discuss an issue or issues of mutual interest or concern.

We want to call attention to one other public education program.

Every so often, an organization undertakes a project of uncertain prospects that turns out to be a winner beyond anyone's most optimistic expectations. The Winthrop Rockefeller Awards for Distinguished Rural Service was that kind of program for the center. It deserves a mention not only because of its success, but principally because it, or a program like it, ought to be and could be continued by any number of other institutions.

The center started the Rockefeller awards program in 1980 after more than two years of consideration by the board of directors and the center staff. Annually, two $10,000 awards were presented. So in three years, six $10,000 awards were presented. In those years, the Winthrop Rockefeller Awards for distinguished Rural Service

- received widespread support from political leaders in all fifty states (Virginia governor Charles S. Robb presented the 1982 awards, and many governors and members of Congress participated in various aspects of the awards);

- were presented by the vice president of the United States in 1981;
- brought added success to the winners' projects through the local and regional publicity resulting from the awards;
- were called "A...Nobel Prize for rural folks" by the *Country Journal* and the "most prestigious award of its kind" by Cornell University;
- had more than four hundred individuals from each of the fifty states nominated for the awards—men and women in all walks of life; and finally
- recognized six talented, devoted, and deserving rural leaders, who brought character, dignity, and their own personal warmth to the program and who became the most convincing argument each year for why we, as a nation, should care about rural people and issues—which was a major reason for instituting the program.

These six outstanding individuals included

MINNIE MILLER BROWN (North Carolina, 1980), who, through her teaching and publications, emphasized the plight of women and poor rural minorities throughout the rural South, helped plan a national food and nutrition program aimed at low-income families, served on a national task force that planned the reporting system for the Expanded Food and Nutrition Education Program, and trained nutrition aides, who were from low-income families and were native to rural areas, so the program could reach remote rural areas and the neediest of families;

ROMAN KETTLER (South Dakota, 1980), who, as agriculture supervisor for the Northeast South Dakota Community Action Program, developed an innovative approach to helping low-income farmers get access to capital

35

and diversify their operations and played an instrumental role in the development of Dakotah Incorporated, an employee-owned sewing corporation that began in 1972 with a sales volume of $30,000 and by 1979 reported sales totaling $6.5 million for the 350 owner-workers;

JOHN D. ANDREWS (Louisiana, 1981), who, as Morehouse Parish horticulture crops and community resource development agent of the LSU Cooperative Extension Service, has helped residents deal with the changing nature of the rural economy, helped start the Bastrop Farmers' Market in 1972 allowing about four hundred black and white families to sell between $450,000 and $750,000 in produce each year, and also contributed to the establishment of a meat and vegetable processing center in 1978;

M. DWAYNE YOST (Kentucky, 1981), founding executive director of the Kentucky Mountain Housing Development Corporation—the second largest producer of new homes in coal-producing eastern Kentucky, offering affordable homes for low-income rural families and training local volunteers for jobs in housing construction and repair—and a leader in developing construction techniques suitable for his rural market and in seeking new technology;

JOHN BROWN, JR. (Alabama, 1982), organizer and president of the South East Alabama Self-Help Association, Inc., which was formed to develop business ventures for jobs and incomes and to provide help for creating and expanding businesses, and which, through its various business activities, community services, and educational assistance, has benefited thousands over a twelve-county area of Alabama since its establishment in 1967; and

ARTURO V. RAMIREZ (Texas, 1982), who in 1970 helped organize and then managed the Military Highway Water Supply Corporation, a cooperative utility that brought the first safe drinking water in over a hundred years to 4,750 families—mainly migrant and seasonal farmworkers—in the rural *colonias* of the lower Rio Grande Valley.

Four factors seem to account for the program's success:
• the decision to seek nominees who had not been recognized previously;
• the decision to keep the nominating procedure simple so as not to discourage potential nominators from submitting names;
• an investment in extensive, independent investigation of the nominees to protect the credibility and integrity of the awards, key to establishing the prestige of the program; and
• the appointment of former Pennsylvania governor Raymond Philip Shafer as the chairman of the independent awards selection panel. As a former governor of a state with a large rural population, Governor Shafer was greatly interested in rural issues and people. He and Winthrop Rockefeller had known each other well and had been governors during the same period of time. From those early planning stages, Governor Shafer became a highly active chairman, instrumental in the direction and decisions of the awards program and in its success. (He was, in fact, so instrumental to the success that he was awarded a special, no cash, Winthrop Rockefeller Award for Distinguished Rural Service unanimously by the board of directors at what turned out to be the final awards presentation in May, 1982.)

However, as crucial as good planning and execution were, they alone do not account for the success of the program. The awards program struck a chord, and it seemed to develop a personality and an emotional presence, perhaps even a character, uniquely its own.

This personality, this character would be felt at several different points. For example, the first year, as the deadline for nominations approached, books, newspaper clippings, and shoe boxes filled with information poured in. From forty-four states came 172 nominations. The response was astounding. Moreover, each year that character and emotional presence was felt in the winners—in their nervousness, sometimes their tears, and their pride and joy, which the center shared. Each year the center would figure the program had peaked. The next year's response and the winners couldn't possibly carry the emotion. Yet it and they always did. It was a curious phenomenon.

In summary, the center did get into a lot of different areas in its six years of existence, perhaps too often in response to opportunities provided by funders. If the center were judged on the basis of pursuing a well-defined set of goals, it is easy to understand why its diverse program obscured its purpose and approach. On the other hand, if it were viewed as what it was—an experimental, evolving organization—the lessons learned and recommendations resulting from the experience can provide the basis for designing a broadly engaged but well-defined organization, which funders seem to prefer.

The examples cited in this section illustrate the synergistic impacts and potential success of the center's concept and strategy.

A demonstration project testing a rural employment outreach model not only resulted in increasing the number of rural minorities trained and hired on several public works projects, but led to the creation of a planning process for the Tennessee-Tombigbee area, design and implementation for economic development programs in four rural areas of the country, the imposition of the first affirmative action hiring programs (including jobs for women) in rural areas, and reports that community-based organizations could use to plan their own strategies.

Monitoring federal health programs led to increased Medicare revenues for rural clinics; increased federal construction dollars for rural clinics; establishment of both a national network of three thousand organizations and individuals and a Washington, D.C., network supportive of rural health programs; meetings between federal regulation writers and rural practitioners affected by the regulations; changes in those regulations; and a widely acclaimed national rural health newsletter.

Publishing a report on rural poverty and public assistance programs led to a White House welfare reform bill responsive to rural problems; an effective lobbying effort on behalf of the bill; background material for a National Academy of Sciences task force; data for other organizations to use in preparing proposals; broader awareness of the existence and nature of rural poverty; and creation of a data base used to analyze and promote changes to a number of other public assistance programs.

Answering requests for information led to assistance for those seeking information; identification of gaps in federal programs; creation of a federal interagency task force; improvements in administration of water and sewer programs; a series of White House rural development initiatives; and creation of a national network of individuals and organizations interested in rural issues.

Former staff members could offer as many additional examples as those listed. For example, the director of the health program spent the better part of two days briefing the House Ways and Means Committee staff and an official of Blue Cross for a committee hearing on the Rural Clinics Act. Two staff members helped a number of community development corporations develop a legislative strategy for design and passage of a bill to give corporations tax deductions for assistance to citizen-based organizations involved in community development activities. Two rural enterprise zone bills, based on data supplied by the center, were introduced in Congress. A graduate course in policy analysis at the University of Minnesota is using a center publication. The staff of the House Agriculture Committee used information and recommendations in *A Rural Banking Facility* in reviewing the status of rural development. And so on, and so on....

FIVE

What We Learned: Some Conclusions

B ecause the purpose of a national rural policy organization would be to influence policy, it is important to refer again to the "policy-making process" discussion in the second chapter. The steps in the process are both formal and informal. The informal part, where issues are first identified and given shape and where potential options are generated, is the point at which a national policy organization should seek to intervene. The nature of the informal part calls for forums that are not public, where options can be examinied thoroughly and there is no rush to premature recommendations. Decision makers can learn about all aspects of an issue and explore a variety of options.

After more than six years, the center learned a lot. And from what it learned we find some suggestions for the future, too.

A. Lessons on the policy process.

Lesson One. Rural development and rural poverty are not priority concerns among national opinion and decision makers. Neither the Carter nor the Reagan administration came into office with a rural development agenda.

The Carter administration eventually approached the question by identifying and seeking to correct "glitches" in federal programs that were supposed to serve rural areas. For example, while several federal health agencies were funding personnel to deliver primary medical care in rural areas, the Farmers Home Administration was not making community facility loans for primary care facilities. Similarly, many rural communities could qualify for neither the Farmers Home Administration's nor the Environmental Protection Agency's water and sewer programs because of funding and project design requirements. Furthermore, regulations governing allocation of public transportation grants were not appropriate for many rural communities. So there were great gaps in performance, resulting from definitions and a lack of understanding. President Carter eventually established a rural policy and program staff within the White House, out of which emerged, with considerable encouragement and pushing from Congress and rural advocacy groups, support for the Rural Development Policy Act of 1980. This act sought to establish within the Department of Agriculture a federal focal point for the collection of data and the review of federal policies affecting rural areas. However, even though the Carter administration announced its support for the bill with some fanfare in December 1979, the legislation did not escape from the Office of Management and Budget (OMB) until the following August. Such a delay prompts questions about the depth of the administration's commitment to the concept, and about whether OMB works for the president or functions as an independent agency accountable to no one.

Congress passed the act by unanimous consent shortly after the administration announced its support. The Reagan administration, however, has made little effort to carry out the letter or spirit of the act. Most senior level political appointees in the Department of Agriculture appear to equate rural with farming, thus ignoring 90 percent of the rural population and the changes occurring in the rural economy. Of course, since the Reagan administration sought to reduce if not eliminate a federal role in local development, its agriculture appointees may have had little choice but to ignore the various barriers to economic development in poor rural areas. Some fifteen months into its term, the Reagan administration did announce formation of a national advisory committee called for by the Rural Development Policy Act. However, the committee was given a very short life and very limited resources for staff and travel. More limiting, the committee kept with the administration's general approach to ignore whatever initiatives had been launched under the Carter administration. It was asked to focus on new and voluntary approaches to rural development, which meant still another period of reexamination, no decisions, and no action.

The lack of interest and understanding, however, is not surprising, for national opinion and decision makers have little appreciation for the national stake in rural areas:

- The Conference Board, the influential research organization serving many of the nation's top corporations, reported that it received few, if any, requests from its members to research any rural development issues. This report prompted a National Rural Center paper entitled *The Corporate Interest in Rural Development* (see appendix), which was circulated to several Conference Board staff members.
- *Newsweek Magazine* featured a cover story on the growth of small towns, which presented a generally idyllic portrait of rural America, ignoring both the problems that too rapid growth created in some small towns and

the continued existence of rural poverty in many rural areas.

• *The Washington Post* treated as major news in 1982 the Census report describing the population growth in rural areas, despite the fact that the historic turnabout had been well documented elsewhere for more than five years.

• *The Washington Post* noted that rural areas were included in a bill to create enterprise zones in economically distressed communities because several farm state senators were on the legislative committee, ignoring the fact that if the concept makes sense, it makes sense as a way to create jobs in economically distressed rural areas, too. The prejudices against rural areas remain.

• Few foundations have an interest in rural development in general or as it affects the rural poor and minorities. Several foundations support various civil rights activities, which are important to minorities in rural areas. By and large, however, these foundations have not recognized, at least not in their funding decisions, that in rural areas access to and control of private sector resources and enterprises are key to maintaining and expanding the rights and freedoms gained through litigation. And, of course, civil rights litigation does not directly affect the majority of the poor rural residents, who are white. Foundations apparently have difficulty dealing with the concept of rural development and policy, for their board and program officers tend to seek narrow and perhaps magical issues where a foundation's giving can have a visible impact (suggesting, perhaps, that all of us need successes, even foundations whose mission it is to attempt that which no other institution can). In addition, foundations tend to shy away from direct efforts to influence policy, to see their role as initiators rather than as long-term funders, and to favor urban over rural concerns. To the extent that foundations help form the national policy agenda, and they do, their reluctance to deal with rural development issues is an important reason why these issues do not receive attention at the national level.

• No influential academic discipline or organization focuses on rural development policy issues. Two major academic societies do focus on important elements but not on the whole of rural development: the American Agriculture Economics Association for the most part is concerned with farm issues, and the Rural Sociological Society (which recently published an impressive collection of essays on the future of rural America) is concerned with rural society in the United States. However, it should not detract from the value of either organization's work to note that most members of both groups are not familiar with the policy process, nor influential in it.

• What little pressure the U.S. Department of Agriculture exerted on the land grant system to give increased attention to rural development issues is disappearing with cutbacks in community development research and extension funds and with increases for work on agricultural issues.

• Conversations with officers of corporations who have customers or resources in rural areas confirmed the general lack of interest in and understanding of rural problems and potentials. In some cases, the lack was a result of the issues never having been brought to their attention; in others, it was a result of the automatic correlation of farming with rural or of a feeling (probably correct) that development might cause labor costs to rise or might lead to more organized efforts to control the way resources were extracted from rural areas.

That rural development and rural poverty are not priority concerns among national opinion and decision makers is not terribly surprising as a lesson. That they should be is the point. The prejudices and misconceptions against rural concerns are deep, widespread, and institutionalized, and that is an important part of the problem.

Lesson Two. The lack of a data base handicaps decision making on rural concerns and fails to provide the support necessary for policy design and advocacy. The corollary is that many nongovernment funders generally do not understand the importance of data and the role data plays in driving policy. They find "data" too neutral or passive, preferring to support direct advocacy, projects located where "the tire meets the road" (whatever that means), or projects that directly create jobs (for how long doesn't always seem to matter). Some government agencies are willing to fund data collection, but too often only for data that will support their programs, their pet theory, or a particular strategy (such as elimination of programs).

These comments do not apply to the Bureau of the Census and other institutionalized government agencies that collect data on a macroscale. They face another kind of problem, particularly as their work affects rural policy. Even before the arrival of Reaganomics, these agencies lacked resources to collect enough data to be statistically relevant in rural areas or to publish useful interpretations of the rural data they had collected. Now, with cutbacks in almost all federal data collection efforts, the information base for rural policy will continue to be inadequate. For example, the size of the sample for the monthly Current Population Survey had been large enough to be statistically significant for the nation and metropolitan areas, but not for nonmetropolitan areas. Rather than enlarge the sample size, the Reagan administration reduced it, perhaps to the point that the figures will be useful only at the national level. One might argue that an administration sincerely intent on balancing the federal budget ought to increase its data collection efforts so as to have a larger information base for economic assumptions and income tax and federal expenditure projections. One should argue that the collection of data is a federal responsibility, which ought to be pursued whatever view one might hold of other proper roles of the federal government.

The academic community, of course, does tend to appreciate the importance of data, though too often its findings are presented for the approval of colleagues and not for use by nonexperts. Academics also tend to discount the value of collecting episodic information on how things really work at the local level, or if they don't discount it, they feel a need to aggregate and "formulize," even though the sample may be small and variations are omitted in the formulation process. Also, they appear reluctant to collect data at the local level without first postulating a theory to be proved or disproved. Granted, that is the traditional approach to research, but it is also an approach that can assume more knowledge than exists about how development occurs and programs work. As a result, research agendas and projects can become separated from and irrelevant to the needs of potential users at the policy-making and implementation levels. For example, many agriculture researchers argue that much of their work is size neutral; i.e., a pesticide will be as effective in protecting an apple tree on a small farm as on a large one. However, they often fail to examine the costs and complexity of applying the pesticide, which may put the technology beyond the reach of a small-farm operator. Or they assume that by merely placing a subsidized medical practice in a medically underserved rural area, the practice will become automatically self-supporting, an assumption that ignores various economic and practice barriers to profit making, which exist in rural areas but not in suburban or metropolitan areas. Or as the center found in a case study of development finance needs, several communities had not used a particular federal program because they were not aware of its existence. That kind of information and aggregate statistics, and data that identify trends and program impacts, are necessary to design and implement effective rural development policies. (For a detailed discussion of rural policy data needs, read *Rural America in Passage: Statistics for Policy*, a report of the National Academy of Science published in 1981.)

Lesson Three. It is difficult, if not impossible, for narrow purpose federal agencies and interest groups to come together, formulate, and carry out coordinated rural policies. Fragmented policies are the result. Federal policies and programs important to rural development are spread over a number of departments and countless agencies within departments. The Departments of Agriculture, Commerce, Defense, Education, Energy, Health and Human Services, Housing and Urban Development, Interior, Labor, Transportation, and the Treasury make policies affecting rural communities. Within the Department of Agriculture, for example, the Farmers Home Administration, the Science and Education Administration, the Cooperative State Extension Service, the Soil Conservation Service, the Forest Service, and the various farm agencies all are involved in issues important to the quality of life in rural areas. But no effective mechanism yet exists for coordinating rural policies and programs, either in agencies within departments or across departments. Narrow visions, concerns for turf, and a lack of agreed-upon definitions and goals are among the barriers to rural policy coordination. This fragmentation is further en-

48

couraged by the dispersion of authorizing and appropriating responsibility among numerous congressional committees and by the narrow focus of special interest groups working their own particular turf. In an admittedly limited way, the experience of the center demonstrated that a low-profile, broadly concerned nongovernment agency can be effective in helping bridge gaps resulting from this fragmentation. What is needed in the area of rural development is what the Center for Strategic and International Studies (CSIS), as described by David M. Abshire, its president, seeks to be in the area of foreign policy:

> The problem with the total decision making process in Washington is its compartmentalization. You get jealousies, you get conflicts of interests, you get bureaucrats who lack effective freedom of action. There's great difficulty of conceptualization. I think outside groups have a very special role to perform at this time which maybe they didn't have in the 1950s. In the 1980s, with the vast number of interest groups, with the Balkanization of America that is occurring, we have a serious problem of organization, strategy, and leadership—and you've got to have all three. . . .
>
> The role of the Center for Strategic and International Studies is to help policy makers get beyond the ideological or parochial preconceptions and see problems in long-range, interdisciplinary perspective. CSIS "attempts to be a bridge between the world of ideas and the world of action. . . . *

Mr. Abshire might have been reading from some material about the National Rural Center.

Lesson Four. Rural people can be organized effectively around particular issues (health, housing, etc.), but probably not around rural development or similar comprehensive concepts (equity, poverty, etc.). Over the years, three

---

* James Lardner, "Thick and Think Tank," *Washington Post,* 21 September 1982, sec B.

general approaches have been taken to organizing people in order to influence national policies important to
rural areas. One approach sought to create and inform
networks of people and organizations interested in a specific rural issue; the second sought to create formal organizations or lobbies to represent particular economic
interests; and the third sought to create national organizations of rural people and to interest Washington groups
under the banner of a broad statement of concerns. The
center was involved in two of those approaches as a creator of informed networks and as a founding member of
the Rural Coalition, which sought to become a voice for
rural community-based organizations. The center also
worked with a number of groups, which represented, with
variations, all three approaches; these groups included
the National Rural Electric Cooperative Association, the
Housing Assistance Council, Rural America, the Congressional Rural Caucus Advisory Team, and the Family Farm
Coalition. The following observations are drawn from the
center's efforts and from the experience of others.

- It is extremely difficult and expensive for an advocacy
coalition committed to "rural development" to set and
stick to priorities. For example, the Rural Coalition,
with a small budget and staff, was continually asked
to be involved in issues of the moment with which its
Washington members were concerned, as well as in
issues suggested from the field, ranging from the MX
Missile to Farmers Home water and sewer programs
to recommendations for a rural development policy. Not
surprisingly, the priority concerns of member organizations varied as to geography, mission, and focus of the
individual community-based organization. Thus, while
a coalition of 250 rural organizations (5 per state) interested in a broad range of development issues would

be an effective lobby, it must be recognized that a process to set priorities and to keep members informed would be lengthy and very costly, particularly if member organizations were to participate fully in the process. Such a coalition would be likely to need an annual budget of $350,000 to $500,000, provided it could rely on members and other organizations for policy research and analysis, a risky assumption at best.

• Networks or organizations formed around a particular issue or interest can attract participants and be effective in narrow fields, whether they are formed around an economic concern (such as the National Rural Electric Cooperative Association [NRECA] or the Association of Land Grant Universities) or around a particular subject (such as delivery of primary health care). If the pool of potential participants is large and/or wealthy enough (milk producers, tobacco growers, and food processors), the organization can limit its members to a narrowly defined pool. But networks interested in rural development issues important to those at the lower end of the economic scale cannot afford that luxury. They need all the help they can get. For example, the center's rural health network of some three thousand persons included practitioners, researchers, advocates, public officials, congressional staff members, and bureaucrats. In addition, the center sought allies on an issue-by-issue basis, operating on the strategy of no permanent friends or enemies. In this way, the center's health network, working with NRECA, was successful in influencing a number of national policies affecting delivery of primary health care in medically underserved rural areas. Whether the network could have been maintained around broader health care issues was not tested, and the center was far less successful in creating networks around other issues for a number of reasons, in-

51

cluding orientation of staff, funding, and subject matter.
• The fragmentation of rural interest groups limits their effectiveness. The desire to create a rural development lobby at the national level, particularly one responsive to the rural poor, is both understandable and correct. Separately, groups interested in health care, housing, and clean water, for example, can have only limited effect; together they could form an impressive coalition. And no one should dispute that all three concerns are inseparably linked when viewed in terms of the well-being of the rural resident or community. The question then is not whether a broad-based rural coalition is desirable, but how one can be created and maintained. Barriers to doing so include funding, the natural preoccupation of individual groups with their own concerns, limited knowledge about the policy process, and the difficulty of working across issues while maintaining credibility with single-purpose organizations.
• Many advocacy groups and technical assistance organizations interested in rural development issues lack an adequate data base to assist themselves and groups in the field to develop policy positions. This shortcoming is the result of organizations' missions, funding limitations, and/or orientation. Given the budgetary, legal, and political restraints on public agencies, the collection, analysis, and dissemination of such information will have to be funded and done by the private sector.

B. Lessons on organizing and managing a national rural policy and information organization.

Lesson One. To encourage an interdisciplinary approach to rural development, the staff should be organized according to functions rather than issues. When the center began operations in March of 1976, its program focused on health, employment and training, and building of a rural development library and information service. As the organization grew, the center kept a subject area approach, eventually having programs in capacity building, economic development (including small farms and development finance), health, human services, and the library. Because of reporting requirements, geography, and personalities, however, it was a continuing struggle to find ways for the programs' areas to relate to each other. The development of projects and activities by subject area made crosscutting approaches difficult. But staff would be required to reach across subject areas if it were organized by functions, such as information collection and analysis, public education, and networks.

Lesson Two. Despite claims to the contrary, most people do not feel comfortable in jobs with less than precise job descriptions. While most of the people hired by the center said they welcomed the opportunity to work for an evolving, crosscutting organization, the vast majority sooner or later requested bureaucratic job descriptions, wage scales, etc., all of which encouraged stratification and departmentalization and discouraged flexibility. It takes intellectually secure individuals to work in an interdisciplinary, multifunctional organization, and those people can be difficult to recruit to nonprofit organizations. In hiring staff, the center erred by decentralizing the recruitment process, by not requiring probationary periods for professionals as well as support staff, and by giving unsatisfactory employees too many chances to develop and change. The latter mistake was the product of a do-good mentality that saw the center in the business of developing individuals as well as serving rural people. An equally if not more compelling argument holds that nonprofit organizations using someone else's money and existing to assist others ought to hold employees to a higher level of competence than profit-making organizations. Maybe the poor would fare better at the national level if the organizations of middle-class folks created to help them took a more professional business approach to their mission.

Lesson Three. The core program should be structured to encourage a comprehensive approach, continuity, and continuously increased knowledge and effectiveness. While the center, thanks to the Winthrop Rockefeller Charitable Trust, enjoyed a useful level of general program support, that support was not enough to fund a comprehensive core program. Rather, the center had to secure support for individual projects. While the various projects were consistent with the center's goals and mission, their ad hoc nature confused the public image of the center, encouraged internal fragmentation, and made development of a permanent core staff difficult. If a center is established in the future, it should be funded to carry out an agreed-upon core program designed to help rural people overcome the various barriers to their participation in the policy process. To be successful, the program must build on itself, so that the knowledge base and the effectiveness of the staff increase over time.

Lesson Four. Federal money should not be accepted for the core program and possibly not for any reason. Federal money is expensive in terms of time spent securing it, time spent collecting it (at one time the federal government was $400,000 in arrears to the center), and time spent filling out reports. Also, with few exceptions, federal agencies do not fund broad-based policy research or analysis, but prefer agency-serving and narrow projects. Further, there is little continuity within agencies, with each new administrator anxious to do his or her thing, whether there is a change of administration in the White House or just a change in the leadership of an agency. On occasion a publicly funded project might be a useful addition to the core program, but care should be taken to make clear that any staff taken on for that project is temporary. Also, the project must be under the control of the core staff.

Lesson Five. The core program should ensure continuing staff contact with grass-roots practitioners, leading thinkers, and decision makers across the country. To ensure that the core program is grounded in practicality, is intellectually sensitive to emerging trends and issues, and is relevant to decision making, the program must require the staff to meet and interact with practitioners, experts, opinion makers, and decision makers across the nation.

Lesson Six. A nonprofit organization seeking to retain a core staff over time faces the twin problems of encouraging productivity and holding down costs. Obviously in a policy development and information organization, labor is the major cost. Unlike a for-profit firm, it is difficult for a nonprofit policy organization to increase charges on services to increase corporate income. Also, once a staff is working full time, additional projects mean almost equal additional costs. However, if a core staff is to be retained, some sort of reward system is required, but one that will not exhaust reserves or price the organization out of the fund-raising market. The center had a policy of awarding cost-of-living raises and merit increases, with the former, because of inflation, far outstripping the latter, which of course diminished the incentive value of merit increases. Further, the combination of merit and cost-of-living increases, even with various ceiling and partial awards based on performance, resulted in steadily escalating costs and project budgets. Therefore, if incentives are needed to retain staff and encourage productivity, nonprofit firms also need incentives for cutting costs.

Lesson Seven. Fiscal management is key to cost control,

sound planning, and insured credibility. Nonprofit organizations must reject the temptation to cut costs when hiring fiscal management staff. Fiscal management is not a necessary evil that "public-interest" groups must endure; it is the basis for running an effective organization, particularly one seeking credibility with a broad range of private and public sector audiences. The center was fortunate in having a skilled finance officer willing to work long hours. She deserved more quality assistance than she received. However, it was a source of pride and, we think, credibility that from start to finish, including the phaseout of the corporation, the center's financial records were complete, clean, and timely. Because of its fiscal management, the center was able to stretch its resources while waiting for new funding, and when the funding did not arrive, it was able to close with all bills paid and to donate its most valuable tangible asset—its rural development library—to Tuskegee Institute.

Lesson Eight. In an era of limited resources, nonprofit organizations need to generate income as well as receive grants and contracts and pursue sophisticated investment strategies. To do both requires sound fiscal management. The ability to generate income does not violate the spirit or purpose of a nonprofit educational organization. To the contrary, the ability can make the organization attractive to potential donors, provide independence and flexibility, and generate resources for fiscal incentive programs. Once a public-interest nonprofit organization overcomes a reluctance to generate income, it needs to determine for which programs, services, and products it can charge. To the extent possible, income-generating activities ought to flow out of an organization's normal program. Charging for newsletters and other publications is an obvious starting point. Another is what we call "information transfer" conferences or seminars, in which an organization could use its expertise (including outside experts) to provide information to a paying audience. For example, the center was exploring the potential of a series of seminars designed to assist state officials and local organizations to adjust to changes in federal rural and community health programs. The key to generating income above costs is to be able to conduct the same seminar several times, thus spreading the cost of planning and developing the program. Given the large number of for-profit organizations apparently making money from information meetings, there appears to be a lively market for such services. Of course, the seminars must appeal to a broader audience than the poor or struggling community-based organizations. It is difficult to make money selling to the poor.

The center also had developed a plan to sell professional reference services to organizations and businesses in Washington. This plan was to be based on the expertise and research resources gained over the years of operating a rural information service. For $12,000 a year, less than the cost of one-half person, the center would have provided clients with a range of research services and access to basic data and documents.

The key to stretching resources through investments of idle funds is to be able to project monthly income and expenditures accurately. With that information, an organization can place funds not needed immediately for expenses into a range of investments coming due at various but appropriate intervals, such as three, six, and twelve months—or longer, depending on resources available. In doing so, the choice of investments should be determined primarily by the return and security and not by other factors.

Lesson Nine. While foundation and government officials have difficulty understanding multipurpose organizations with broad agendas, the more serious problem (provided funds are available) is making certain that employees understand the breadth and limits of the mission. Like everyone else, employees of multipurpose, public-interest organizations bring their own definitions, visions, and agendas with them. In an evolving organization, one should probably expect employees to put their own interpretation on the mission of the organization and its role. Unfortunately, these variations can unnecessarily blur the image of the organization, internally as well as externally. As noted previously, funders generally have enough trouble understanding an interdisciplinary, multipurpose organization without receiving mixed signals from the staff. Also, incorrect or exaggerated expectations can be generated among the people with whom the organization works. And internally, such uncertainty can generate endless rounds of discussions, inappropriate project ideas, and a lack of cohesiveness. In the case of the center, a great deal of staff tension was created over the question of whether it was in the technical assistance business. If so, to what degree, and what did the term mean, anyway? In a sense, the dissemination of information of any kind is a form of technical assistance, so technically the center was in the business. However, it was not the center's principal mission to deliver how-to advice, though it did some of that to learn, gain contacts, and provide service. Instead, its basic concern was with the policies and programs that determined the amount and kinds of technical assistance provided by the private and public sectors.

Lesson Ten. Regional offices are expensive to administer effectively. The center had two regional offices, which started as offices associated with a particular project. Regional offices can provide important access to rural residents and experts of the region as well as conduct projects that could not be run from Washington. On the other hand, they are expensive to maintain, and they tend to feel isolated or overly important (as the ones closest to the firing line) unless adequate funds are available to allow constant staff travel to and from the national office. A well-designed core program that insures staff contact with a range of practitioners and thinkers diminishes the need for regional offices, particularly if the organization is not in the business of seeking a raft of individual projects. A national rural policy organization with a core budget of between $1 million and $2 million cannot afford regional offices.

Lesson Eleven. Selecting a diversified board of directors may be more difficult than it would seem initially. Funding sources look at leadership, including the board of directors, when considering organizations for grants. The stated purpose of a board of directors is to assure the fiduciary integrity of an organization. A board's responsibilities include policies on revenues, investments, expenditures, general management, and the general-to-specific program directions of the corporation as a whole. When dealing with national rural development policy, a board should have regional, ethnic, political, and professional diversity. It should have representatives from business, labor, academia, and government, including state and local governments. It should have representatives from grass-roots, community-based organizations and nationally recognized figures. It should have directors who are articulate and well informed on broad national policy problems as well as on more specific regional and local problems. A board should be large enough in its membership to accommodate diversity and small enough to assure reasonable expenditures for at least two meetings a year. Finally, a board is said to need among its members those who can raise substantial sums of money on a peer-to-peer basis, presumably easily and quickly and apparently at no expense to the member's own projects, programs, or commitments.

If selecting such a board in the largely experimental rural development policy field is possible, we concede that the center never quite pulled it off. The center's board met the tests of diversity. It understood the complexity of rural issues and set corporate policies accordingly. It understood that successful ventures as models might do as much toward the elimination of poverty as anything else. Finally, it worked well as a unit and was exceptionally loyal to the concept of a rural center and its staff. On nearly each criterion, the center's board consistently met the tests. The one exception was fund-raising.

Fund-raising "clout," as it was occasionally described, was a late arrival to the criteria list and in our view may be in conflict and inconsistent with the constituency and mission of the organization. If rural people and issues had clout, would a rural center be needed in the first place? There is one additional problem. Funders tend to change what they view as appropriate board make-ups without warning. That is understandable for government agencies when administrations change. It is less understandable when foundations suddenly criticize an organization for a board of directors that had been selected to meet their criteria.

Lesson Twelve. It is difficult to educate and sell at the same time. With an experimental concept, it may be impossible. Educating requires a certain level of information, and attention to details may be most important when misconceptions are widespread, as they are on rural issues. Selling probably requires brevity and a certainty of direction. It assumes a particular and hopefully accurate information base and point of reference. But what if both are generally inaccurate? A certain level of education may be required before selling is even reasonably possible.

60

SIX

Some Suggestions For the Future

Our program, organizational, and management recommendations are driven by the following concerns, as shaped by lessons from the past.

Increased competition for development resources. Regardless of shifts in political winds, public resources for domestic development programs will be in short supply for the next decade or longer, and the private sector (including private foundations) will not make up the cutbacks in federal dollars, let alone the difference between need and supply. If rural people and areas are to compete successfully for a share of available resources, their needs and potentials will have to be presented credibly and forcefully to the informal and formal parts of the policy-making process. *That means a national rural policy program must be concerned with education and advocacy.*

Dealing with change. The economy of the United States is changing from one based on cheap energy to one based on expensive energy, from one predominantly oriented to manufacturing to one increasingly oriented to services. The nation's population is aging and moving. Large numbers of people seek smaller scale places in which to live and work and sometimes are willing to trade earning potential for quality of life considerations. New technology makes possible if not encourages diffusion of economic activity and places new demands on our educational and job-training programs. Persistent economic stagnation damages, perhaps even negates, old economic theories, and no one knows for sure if unacceptable rates of inflation are dead or just temporarily dormant. The nation's physical infrastructure wears out at an alarming rate, which means that repair as well as new construction must be financed. There is broader appreciation of the critical role small and young businesses play in creating new jobs, but limited experience exists on how to significantly increase the rates of starts and successes. Innovative and increased private-public sector cooperation and ventures are called for, but only limited recommendations for achieving them are offered. Most people agree the nation needs a mix of farm sizes and ownership patterns, but national policies continue to encourage larger and larger farm operations and to work against the viability of medium- to small-family farms. That partial list suggests the extent of unknowns facing decision makers in the 1980s. *Therefore, a national rural policy organization must be as concerned with identifying pragmatic approaches, documented by local experience, as with overall trends and aggregated statistics.*

Fragmented policy-making process. Regardless of how effectively the Rural Policy Act of 1980 may be implemented eventually (if it doesn't expire because of neglect during the next two years), federal policies and programs important to rural development will continue to be spread among many agencies with no effective means for coordination. Also, there is no reason to assume continuity of efforts between administrations or even between administrators. Further, the growth in the number and influence of special interest groups increases pressures to fragment the policies. And finally, the need for increased private-public sector cooperation makes coordinated approaches even more important. *That means a national rural development policy organization must be a data base that drives policies within and across departments, an easily accessible source of data for private and public sector decision makers, and a catalyst for bringing private and public decision makers together around a rural development agenda.*

Incentives and the nonprofit organization. Just as rural development practitioners will find increased competition for funds, so too will nonprofit policy organizations. If the policy organization also seeks to maintain a core staff to insure an institutional memory and increased expertise over time, it faces the challenge of rewarding performance and encouraging efficiency without pricing the organization out of existence through salary increases. *That means a national rural policy organization ought to generate some of its own income to demonstrate to funders a demand for its services and products and to support a financial incentive program for employees.*

Other suggestions to consider in designing a future rural center:

- Take no federal money, because it is seldom worth the hassle and costs and may damage credibility with succeeding administrations.
- Hire all staff carefully and on a six-month trial basis because it will be difficult to find staff at ease with and effective in an interdisciplinary, team approach.
- Expand carefully, if at all, beyond the core program, making certain that the project staff understand their employment and project ends at the same time and leave demonstration projects to others.
- Locate in Washington, D.C., where most national decision makers live, visit, or are represented. It is also

an excellent location from which to organize and inform networks, and it has excellent information resources.

• Be willing to provide information to and work with shifting alliances of organizations regardless of individual political persuasions, affiliations, levels of activity, or particular bias; but spend little time on the politics of the Washington-based, do-good world, which can be narrowly focused, survival-oriented, and dominated by process concerns to the point of exhaustion.

• Eschew shrillness, resist signing group statements (write your own if the desire to go public is overwhelming), and be willing to give others credit for your ideas and work, because the opposite can damage long-term credibility resulting in few, if any, short-term gains. The center followed this rule with some success and an occasional misunderstanding.

• Make certain the core program requires staff to visit and work with a broad range of people in rural areas and to interact with outside experts.

The recommended program assumes an endowment of $10 million or assured annual grants totaling $1.1 million, and activities that would generate an additional $400,000 a year income. It entails three overlapping functions: information collection, information analysis, and information dissemination, which includes education and advocacy. The individual components are as follows:

1. The rural development impact assessment project.

Rationale. Particularly in a time of broad changes, it is important to know the impacts of approaches to rural development at the local level. Why do some rural communities develop, while others do not? Can establishment of a primary health care clinic spur additional job creation efforts, and if so, how? Have recent changes in federal programs resulted in decreased or increased development activity? Without such information, decision makers at every level of activity are forced to guess about program impacts, reforms, and initiatives.

Methodology. Ten rural labor markets would be selected to represent the diversity found in rural America. Secondary data for each area on employment, poverty, health status, education, etc. would be collected and then field visits conducted to document local development efforts. Initial focus could be on efforts to create jobs, deliver health care, and provide housing, for example. Public and private sector activities would be documented.

Products. The products would be an information base on local experience, a framework for policy analysis, policy recommendations, and reports on development efforts which could provide lessons for other communities.

2. The rural minorities project.

Rationale. Because for decades minorities migrated from rural to urban areas, public attention has focused on the very real problems of minorities in metropolitan areas. Even with the reversal of that trend nationally, little attention is paid to the status of minorities in rural areas. It is little appreciated, for example, that one of every four blacks and one of every seven Hispanics live in rural areas, and that by almost every economic or social indicator these rural minorities trail rural whites (i.e., 33 percent of rural black families are poor as opposed to 26 percent of Hispanic families and 9 percent of rural white families). It is doubtful that problems of minorities in rural areas will be adequately addressed until the problems are brought to the public's attention and a data base to support policy recommendations is compiled.

Methodology. Beginning with the 1970 and 1980 census data and using other secondary data as it becomes available, trends in migration, income, poverty, employment, housing, business ownership, education, and health status would be identified and documented. Information from field interviews with rural minority leaders would augment the secondary data.

Products. The products would be a periodic publication updating trends affecting rural minorities and a data base for public education, for briefing decision makers, and for devising and justifying policy recommendations.

3. Rural policy seminars and scholars project.

Rationale. A lack of understanding of the national stake in viable rural communities, metropolitan biases in many national policies, a fragmented policy-making process, and an inability to relate impacts of macrotrends and policies on rural areas are barriers to creation and implementation of successful approaches to rural development. To help lower these barriers, a broad range of decision and opinion makers who can influence the informal part of the national policy-making process must be educated about rural potentials and problems.

Methodology. Through a series of two- or three-day seminars (perhaps four a year), the project would bring together researchers, policy makers, and practitioners to examine emerging issues of importance to rural development. A knowledegable person would be funded to prepare a state-of-the-art and critical choices paper for each seminar. The scholar's paper would be augmented by data from the center's various information collection projects.

Products. The products would be a mechanism for bringing together around a rural agenda the knowledge of the academy, the influence of the policy maker, the experience of the practitioner, and the concern of the community; a network of leaders better informed about rural problems and potentials; and an annual publication on critical issues facing rural areas over the next two to ten years (consisting of the scholars' papers and supporting material).

4. Status of rural America project.

Rationale. A lack of data on trends and on levels of well-being in rural areas is one reason why rural development issues do not receive adequate attention at the national level. Without such information, policy makers have no reason to act, no way to set priorities, and no base from which to devise appropriate strategies and programs. Similarly, rural organizations lack information on which to plan sound proposals and around which to organize effective efforts to influence policies. In some cases, the data is just not collected. However, in many other instances, the information is collected but not analyzed or publicized from a rural or rural policy perspective.

Methodology. Statistics on population, employment, income, poverty, age, education, health status, housing, political participation, tax bases, transportation services, capital availability, etc., would be gathered. The sources would include census reports, county business patterns, the current population survey, the annual housing survey, reports from the National Center for Health Statistics, the Social Security Administration's continuous work history sample, unemployment reports, etc. Also using information collected from its other projects, the center would publish a statistical profile of rural America every two years, documenting trends in key areas of concern and highlighting critical issues identified through the seminars project. Statistics would be enriched by selected case studies from the rural development impact assessment project and by insights gained from the rural minorities project. A committee of nationally recognized leaders would advise on the project and help disseminate the results.

Products. The products would be a biennial report on the status of rural America, which would call attention to priority concerns and provide a justification for action;

a mechanism for calling national attention to rural issues; and a data base for analyzing policy recommendations on a continuing basis and for serving decision makers and rural organizations.

5. State briefings on rural trends and issues.

Rationale. With cutbacks in federal support for development programs, additional responsibilities placed on state governments, and a need for greater private-public sector cooperation, it is critical that leaders of these sectors in individual states have a common understanding of trends, issues, and potentials affecting rural communities in their states.

Methodology. Working with interested organizations and officials (i.e., state government offices, development groups, higher education institutions, business leaders, congressional or Senate offices), the center would organize one-day briefings on state rural trends and problems to be held in the state. Briefings would be provided by staff and by national and in-state experts identified by the staff. Costs of briefings could be offset by participation fees or grants from one or more in-state sponsors.

Products. The products would be data reports on individual states and state networks of decision makers better informed about rural issues.

6. Networks.

Rationale. Having the right information and/or right people convinced at the right time are essential to influencing the national policy-making process. Unfortunately, at least from the viewpoint of rural people seeking to influence that process, there are countless decision-making pressure points important to policies affecting rural development. Further, because of their diversity and diffusion, it is difficult to organize rural people effectively around a broad agenda of issues. Nevertheless, rural concerns will continue to be slighted until rural interests are effectively organized to make their concerns known at the national level. Experience suggests that the proper approach is to organize rural people around specific and tangible concerns, with logic suggesting that a broader constituency can be created eventually by joining the different constituencies around common concerns.

Methodology. The center would create and inform networks made up of people and organizations with a particular concern (health care, development finance, family farms, etc.). Participants would be asked to support their particular network by subscribing to a sharply focused newsletter. Bulletins on issues and legislative alerts would be provided free of charge. The newsletters would include, however, reports of interest from other subject areas.

Products. The product would be a rural constituency informed about particular issues and eventually educated to broader concerns.

7. Rural reference service.

Rationale. A national rural policy organization needs a strong reference collection and capability to support its information collection and analysis projects, to create a data base to support rural development policy recommendations, and to be a source of credible and timely information for decision makers. Further, it is important to have an accessible repository for unpublished papers, conference reports, and nontraditional research on rural development issues. And finally, by charging certain types of clients for reference services, the activity could generate significant income.

Methodology. A collection of general reference material and publications on specific rural development issues would be built. It would have a computer capability to perform bibliographic and data searches, including accessing various census tapes. Because of the general as well as the specific nature of the collection and accessible data banks, the service could be marketed to nonrural as well as rural clients.

Products. The products would be an institutional memory for the organization, a systematically expanding rural development data base, a capacity to gain access to and gain credibility with policy makers, and a potential for generating income.

8. Administration.

The final component would embrace general administration, business development activities, and organizational public relations.

While the core program has been described in terms of its individual components, it is a coordinated approach to devising and promoting rural development policies, as can be seen by examining the components in terms of functions and the concerns described at the beginning of this chapter.

By functions, the program breaks down as follows:

Information collection. Rural development impact assessment project, rural minorities project, rural scholars project, status of rural America project, state briefings and reference collection.

Information analysis. Assessment project, the minorities project, the status project, and reference service.

Information dissemination. Publications, networks, newsletters, briefings, project advisory committees, seminars, testimony, responses to requests for information, and advocacy.

The program responds to expressed concerns as follows:

Influencing informal policy-making process. Seminars, state briefings, minorities project, and rural status report.

Influencing formal policy-making process. Networks,

newsletters, response to requests for information, reference service, and advocacy.

Identifying trends. Minorities project, scholars project, biennial report, and state briefings.

Creating a base of documented local experience. Assessment project and minorities project.

Data to drive policy. Assessment project, minorities project, scholars project, and rural status report.

Accessible data resources. Reference service.

Catalyst for convening private and public sector decision makers. Seminars, project advisory committees, state briefings, and ad hoc issue discussions.

Generating income. State briefings, newsletters, reference services, and publications.

Ensuring staff contact with rural practitioners and outside experts. Assessment project, minorities project, scholars project, and state briefings.

The core program is cumulative in that it builds on itself. For example, the assessment, minorities, and scholars projects become part of the status report on rural America and the reference service's data base. The seminars, state briefings, and reference service help gain credibility and access to decision makers. The networks create outside support for policy recommendations. The data and recommendations developed as part of other projects provide information to help increase effectiveness of networks. Etc.

However, describing and pricing the components separately may be helpful in raising money since private foundations tend to prefer supporting a definable project or activity rather than providing overall support. The components of the proposed program would cost annually, in 1982 dollars:

A.	Rural development impact assessment project	$ 300,000
B.	Rural minorities project	100,000
C.	Rural seminars and scholars project (4 of each)	300,000
D.	Status of rural America project	100,000
E.	State briefings on rural trends and issues (5)	125,000
F.	Networks and newsletters (2)	175,000
G.	Rural reference service	250,000
H.	Administration, business development, public relations	150,000
	TOTAL	$1,500,000

A budget of that amount could support a staff organized as follows:

> Executive director
> Special assistant to the director
> Chief of research and analysis
> Senior rural development analyst (3)
> Director of seminars and scholars
> Seminars research assistant and coordinator
> Minorities analyst
> Chief of information
> Director of networks and briefings
> Director of reference service
> Assistant librarian
> Reference service analyst
> Manager of publications
> Staff writer
> Chief of administration/controller
> Finance officer
> Office manager
> Word processing operator
> Secretaries (4)
> Secretary/receptionist

This staff configuration avoids subject specialists and encourages the team approach. For example, the three senior rural development analysts would be from different fields of expertise (economic development, development finance, health care and other services, education and job training, etc.), but they would work as a team on the rural development assessment projects, serve as resources for the seminars, have input on the rural status report, participate in state briefings, and write articles for newsletters. The director of networks and briefings would use information from the impact assessment project, the seminars, and the minorities project. And so on and so on.

A line item budget could be as follows:

Salaries	$ 720,000
Fringe benefits (20%)	144,000
Rural scholars (4)	40,000
Direct costs	305,000
Newsletter production	25,000
Printing (other)	25,000
Travel	100,000
Library material	15,000
Seminars/meetings	120,000
Business expenses	6,000
TOTAL	$1,500,000

Obviously such a budget is somewhat conjectural and does not reflect start-up costs and reduced salary expenditures during the first year of operation. It is offered, however, as an example of how $1.5 million might be allocated and as the basis for suggesting how a financial incentive program and investment schedule might work.

We'll assume the organization is launched with a $10 million endowment. Annual income targets could be:

From endowment	$1,100,000
Newsletters	150,000
Reference service	200,000
Briefings	50,000
Publications	10,000
TOTAL	$1,510,000

Amounts by which expenses fall below and amounts by which generated income exceeds budget targets could then be made available for salary increases. Salaries could be raised temporarily, with the increases paid over several months, after which salaries would revert back to or close to their original base. Regardless of the amount of the increases, basic salaries would be used for allocating program component costs and determining budgets for additional projects. When additional projects result in increased direct costs, new budget targets would be set to determine the amount of money available for financial incentives. On the other hand, to the extent that new projects, through overhead and other line item allocations, decrease the drain on the core budget, that amount could be included in the salary increase pool. And, of course, an organization with the strength of its conviction could use the same process to lower salaries if expenditures exceed and generated income falls below targets.

Further, with sound expenditure projections and tight budget controls, an organization could stretch dollars through investments of varying maturities. Let's assume a constant rate of monthly expenditures and income. Under the suggested budget, that would mean a gross monthly expenditure of $125,000 ($1.5 million divided by twelve) minus a monthly income of $33,000 ($400,000 divided by twelve), for a net monthly spending rate of $92,000.

More than $1 million annually could be generated in interest from an endowment of $10 million.

Perhaps that point can be best illustrated by a sample and possible first-month investment schedule.

Capital Available

Endowment	$10	million
Short-term investment and		
operating capital	1.057	million
Total available for long-term investment	$8.943	million

First-Month Investment Schedule

Operating capital for three months, $276,000 ($92,000 x 3), is earmarked for a repurchase account.

Type	Amount	Rate	Interest
Repurchase	$ 276,000	8%	$ 2,760
3 - months	276,000	9%	6,210
6 - months	505,000	10%	25,250
12 - months	8,943,000	11%	983,730
Interest			
income			$1,017,950

SEVEN

Who Should Care?

E ven accepting the lessons learned and applauding the recommended program and concept, one could and probably should ask if the package is worth an investment of $10 million. Who should care if such an institution exists and why? Rather than resurrect rhetoric from more speeches and proposals than we care to remember, we will offer a list and hope the reader will fill in the gaps.

- Corporate business and banking officials and entrepreneurs, because rural areas (with a population of 60 million and growing) offer markets, locations for enterprises, and living conditions attractive to workers and managers.
- Rural residents who want to increase economic opportunities and/or maintain or improve the quality of life in their communities.
- Urban leaders who want balanced economic growth to avoid a new flood of rural immigrants.
- Foundations, interest groups, and others who are concerned with reducing the level of poverty in the nation (more than 30 percent of the nation's poor live in rural areas).
- Foundations, interest groups, and others who are concerned about sound housing, clean water, good

education, prevention and treatment of illness, etc., because rural areas are home to more than their share of the problems.

• Foundations, interest groups, and others who are concerned about protecting and expanding civil rights for minorities, because discrimination in rural areas remains a major barrier for minorities, who lag behind rural whites and national averages in every category of well-being (poverty rates, income, literacy, morbidity, etc.).

• Farmers and interest groups who are concerned about a diverse agricultural sector, because the availability of nonfarm income is crucial if median and smaller family farms are to survive.

• Bureaucrats who need assistance relating narrow program responsibilities to broader rural development concerns and realities.

• Members of Congress who need access to data documenting recommendations responsive to rural realities.

• Researchers who need encouragement and support to explore rural development issues.

• Thinkers who understand that the availability of options is critical to the well-being of a free society.

• Decision makers who are concerned with the quality of decisions coming from a fragmented policy-making process that is increasingly buffeted by single-purpose pressure groups.

• Policy makers who are interested in any of the above items. As Kenneth M. Martin of Senior Staff Associates, Small Town Emphasis Program, Harrisburg, Pennsylvania, wrote to the center in 1981, "It is important to have an objective, third-party viewpoint on the status and development of those activities which directly affect small rural communities. Your services would be jeopardized if they were provided directly by the federal government or a specific interest group. It is important that a broad-based organization such as NRC continues to provide the research and informational services which can be utilized by smaller, more geographically specific organizations such as ours.''

To those sold on the concept but who suggest that the first $10 million ought to be invested in creating such an institution to deal with urban development policies, we pause . . . and then acknowledge that more than one or even two such organizations are justified. For example, if the resources were available, several organizations could be created to consider the range of development issues affecting various groups of foreign nations or the elderly. Further, we would suggest the creation not of rural and urban development policy centers, but of centers for the study and advancement of microdevelopment policies, with one organization focusing on smaller communities and the other on larger cities, and there is no need to worry about overlap when smaller meets larger.

EIGHT

What Finally Happened And Why

How the National Rural Center came to close may be as important a lesson for planners and funders considering a new national rural policy organization as any other lesson learned from the center's experiences. To say the center closed because it ran out of money is accurate, if not especially illuminating. After all, the center did its best to avoid that unhappy condition, though the result stemmed, in part, from a proper decision of the board of directors.

First, however, if what follows is to have any credibility at all, let us put several statements on the record. While this part of the report necessarily deals with decisions of others not to fund the center, the final responsibility for not selling the center's program rests with the president alone (Cornman), as do the decisions that, lumped together, put too much effort into seeking federal funds. In addition, perhaps operations should have been scaled back sooner to stretch available resources, though there is no particular reason to believe that new funds would have been generated during the time purchased with such a strategy. And finally (demonstrating that there is obviously a limit to his capacity for self-criticism), the president takes some pride in having kept the center open as long as it was and closing it with all bills paid.

With that said, let us review the decisions made and not made that led to the center's closing.

In 1980, acting on the strong recommendation of the president, the center's board of directors voted that the center should seek funding for a coordinated core program rather than for a collection of unrelated contracts or grants. The board agreed that the center ought to exist as an institution pursuing a mission and not as a grants seeker in search of a purpose. It was clear even then not only that the more difficult choice had been made, but also that long-term support would have to come primarily from private foundations.

Prior to that decision, the center had not pursued an aggressive, programmatic, fund-raising strategy with foundations, relying instead on its start-up gifts and project grants and contracts to support its activities. It was believed that foundations would not be interested until the bequest from the Winthrop Rockefeller Charitable Trust was spent and that the best way to secure foundation support would be to demonstrate a record of achievement. The former belief was correct; the latter, probably naive.

The fund-raising strategy, adopted in 1980, encompassed the following efforts:

- a two-year effort to raise $800,000 to $1 million in assured annual funding, principally from foundations;
- continued program activity at a reduced but still credible level, supported by resources on hand, federal grants and contracts, and assorted small project grants;
- a corporate fund-raising effort to be launched once a future program had been assured; and
- several income-generating activities to be phased in during the second year of the fund-raising program.

What happened to that grand strategy follows.

Federal strategy. As 1981 began, the center had verbal commitments from federal agencies totaling up to $600,000. None were delivered.

An office in the Department of Labor had promised $75,000 continued support for the center's rural information service in August 1980, but it never managed to have the papers signed until January 1981. Not surprisingly, the new administration rescinded the grant the following month.

In the fall of 1980, a new director of the Office of Technical Assistance, Economic Development Administration (EDA) held back the agency's normal support for the information service while agency priorities were to be reassessed. By the time that process was completed in the spring of 1981, a new administration was in the White House, the agency's budget had been reduced, and a rural information service was no longer of interest.

The rural information service had been supported by a consortium of federal agencies, with EDA as the coordinating agency through which the funds were collected and allocated. In August 1980, it was agreed that the coordinating agency responsibility should be shifted to the Department of Agriculture in general and perhaps to the Cooperative State Extension Service (CSES) in particular. Discussions with CSES began immediately and always were positive. However, it was not until April 1982, almost two years later, that the Extension Service formally agreed to become the coordinating agency—far too late to be of assistance. In the meantime, several grants from other agencies could not be accepted because of the absence of a lead agency for the consortium.

The center had performed two major projects for EDA's Office of Research: one resulted in a definitive book on balanced growth policies of European nations; the other, in a major report on the nature of the rural economy. In the fall of 1980, the office and the center began discussions about a third major rural economic development study to be funded the following spring, but a change in agency leadership, priorities, and funding made those discussions moot.

Discussion with a new deputy assistant secretary of commerce in the spring of 1982 sums up the risks of depending on federal grants and contracts. After she listened to a rather long description of our program, her first question was why had the center signed a letter with other organizations protesting certain budget cuts made by the Reagan administration. It turned out that the center had not signed the letter (the center rarely signed such missiles, preferring to make its case in its own words), but it had prepared an analysis of the impacts the cuts had on health programs serving the rural poor (the poor were not well served). The distinction was not recognized. More revealing was the fact that while she knew of the letter, she was still so new to the job that, as we left her office, she asked for directions to the department's auditorium.

This litany is presented not to blame others, for again, such actions are to be expected when administrations change, and approvals of these grants would not have assured the long-term viability of the center. It is offered instead to emphasize that government agencies usually are interested in short-term projects, seldom in supporting institutions. At best, they are unreliable sources of funding, which should be looked to only to supplement programs otherwise supported.

Corporate strategy. The center began developing a corporate fund-raising program in May 1980, with a visit to the Conference Board, a research organization for large corporations, followed by preparation of an article on the corporate stake in a viable rural economy (see appendixes). Later, center officials met with a number of company representatives in Washington, D.C., and corporate officials in home offices to test material developed for corporate fund-raising. Given that corporations tend to give small donations repeated over time, it was immediately clear that the effort ought to wait until the center's future was assured so that corporate gifts would be an addition to an ongoing program. Without that assurance, it made no sense for corporations to provide and the center to accept small gifts. In the event that adequate funding became available, the center was prepared with lists, personal contacts, material, events, and proposals for a corporate fund-raising effort.

Income generation strategy. In 1980, the center began charging for some of its publications, and in 1981 it converted its free *Rural Health Newsletter* to a subscription basis. Publication charges were phased in to ensure the center was not charging for products paid for by federal funds. In general, charges for publications were set to recover design, printing, and distribution costs.

The subscription health newsletter was supported entirely by the center's own resources and was designed to eventually produce revenue in excess of costs. The three-year goal was for three thousand subscriptions at subscription rates of thirty-five to forty-eight dollars a year.

The center also prepared a business development plan and material to promote a Professional Reference Service, using the expertise of the staff and resources of the library. Prospective clients included government contractors, consulting firms, corporate planning and government relations executives, associations and interest groups, state and local government agencies, and large public-interest groups. Certain kinds of requests from rural groups were to be handled free of charge. The material was tested on several prospective clients and one customer was signed up. A marketing plan was prepared and submitted to a foundation's program-related investment office, but the request for a business development loan could not be considered until the foundation approved a program grant—which it never did.

Foundation strategy. While the center sought multi-year funding for a core program (outlined previously), the program entailed a series of related but individual projects. Information about the center and its proposed program was sent to fifteen foundations in March of 1981. Foundations were asked to provide general support or to fund a particular project or activity. The information made clear that without new support, the center would close.

In addition, a major foundation already was considering a proposal to fund the proposed Rural Seminars and Scholars Program, a key element of the core program. Overall, the response was less than overwhelming, but somewhat encouraging.

A second major foundation responded by arranging several meetings with its staff to discuss the center, its record, and its plans for the future. It hired an outside consultant to evaluate the center's performance and potential, and it provided an interim grant to help keep the doors open until funding decisions were made. We understand that the report of the consultant was positive, but that is not known for certain. Despite the center's cooperation in the review and requests for a copy, the foundation never shared the report.

Meanwhile, the first foundation continued to send cautious signals about approving the seminars and scholars request, but the schedule for presenting the proposal to the board kept slipping.

Matters moved slowly at both foundations. At one,

84

wholesale staff changes disrupted continuity and interest and slowed decisions; at the other, new board members requested program reviews. It took time. For them, time was time. For us, time was depleting resources.

Several smaller foundations invited specific proposals related to our program. One even invited two. None were funded.

With dwindled resources, it was clear that new funding would have to be approved by May 1982 or the center would have to close.

By early May prospects looked like this:

The seminars proposal was scheduled to be voted on that month. If that or some other major grant were approved, an additional $500,000 would have been sought from the Winthrop Rockefeller Charitable Trust, a third foundation would have allocated an already approved grant of $75,000 for a continuing project, and the consortium of federal agencies supporting the information service would have been reactivated (the Extension Service having just agreed to be the coordinating agency). Those funds would have allowed the center to operate at a useful level of activity and would have provided time to launch its corporate fund-raising program and income-generating plans as well as to continue its effort to secure foundation support.

For reasons never officially explained, the scholars and seminars proposal was not presented to the foundation's board. Indeed, the center was never notified in writing that the proposal was not to be considered. The staff of the foundation that had commissioned the consultant's study then let it be known, through a third party, that it was no longer interested in the center's future. The center was never told why.

With these nondecisions, the other funding possibilities evaporated, and the center closed.

A post mortem seems in order, if for no other reason than to help prevent a future rural policy organization from being plagued by inaccurate memories of the expired center.

It seems clear now that the center was caught in the turbulence of change resulting from the election of 1980, and it did not have the resources, clout, or skill to ride out the storm.

Why the political appointees of the Carter administration did not deliver on their commitments before election day 1980 remains a mystery. Perhaps they thought Carter would win and there would be time to fund projects later. If so, they were at least consistent with past performances in their ability to gauge political trends. Indeed, just a week before the election, a member of the White House staff asked if Cornman would be interested in being appointed to a position in the next Carter administration. For several reasons, including that the position was currently held by an admired friend, Cornman suggested that any such discussion at least wait until after the election.

At any rate, once a new party had captured the White House and Senate, it quickly became clear that the political appointments on their way out of office were no match for bureaucrats interested in preserving options for their new bosses. Under the rules of the political game, it is difficult to argue that the bureaucracy acted improperly, even though receipt of several federal grants might have helped convince foundations that the center was a viable organization.

The politics behind the foundations' decisions is more complex.

To begin with, the foundation world was being swamped by a huge increase in requests for funds from hundreds, if not thousands, of nonprofit organizations losing federal support because of budget cuts and priorities ordered by the Reagan administration. For most of these groups, the federal trough dried up rapidly. Few if any of the foundations, large or small, were equipped with staff or procedures to sort out the large number of requests prudently or efficiently.

Not surprisingly, the rules of the policy research/advocacy foundation game changed as swiftly as the allegiances of the bureaucracy. For examply, where foundations had wanted boards of directors consisting of grass-roots people and experts, they now wanted more movers and shakers who could help attract corporate dollars. Where they had wanted nonprofit organizations to distribute information and services free or inexpensively to community-based organizations and grass-roots leaders, they now favored those that could generate at least some income. Where foundations had been interested in government programs and policies assisting minorities and the poor, they now were interested in enterprise and small business development as the answer to creating jobs and opportunities for the poor. The center was clearly behind the curve on the first two changes and only slightly involved in the third. Again, a good case can be made for the changes, though the speed with which foundations embraced they new faith was a bit disconcerting.

In addition to trying to stay afloat in the general turbulence of change, the center carried some baggage of its own, starting with its subject matter and its concept.

Rural development issues, never high on the foundation world's agenda, sank even lower as staffs and boards tried to sort out priorities from the deluge of new applicants. Also, it was not the time to sell new concepts. Foundations remained interested not in organizations or programs concerned with process, but in projects with visible, tangible products. Many still harbored the dream of investing enough resources in a narrowly defined field to make a measurable, significant contribution to that field.

And finally, the center never quite escaped its past. The decision of the Clark Foundation not to fund the center six years earlier continued to confuse some potential funders. Others were leery of working with an organization established with "Rockefeller money," and still others felt that if the center were worth saving, some other funder ought to take the first step. In many ways, despite the absence of outside accountability, foundations are as turf-conscious as any government bureaucracy.

These then were the center's mistakes and the political realities that led to the center's closing, at least as best as we can determine. The effort to keep the center alive was a curious if not a very unappealing experience. Negotiations with funders, perhaps as a result of the general uncertainty created by the political turbulence, were conducted by indirection, inflection, and innuendo. Word would reach the staff through third parties that this was right or that was wrong. Staff morale rose and dipped with each rumor about the center or its program, and dipped some more as each new delay resulted in an ever-decreasing staff. No doubt many of the criticisms were valid (indeed, we could have offered some far more damaging), but the criticisms never were directed to the center firsthand.

However, all personal sensitivities aside, extenuating circumstances at least explained the causes for the negative decisions, which brings us back to the reason for preparing this report. Despite the plaintive note that creeps in from time to time, we write not to lament but to inform. The failure to patch together financial support from a number of different sources while conducting a program reaffirms the wisdom of the original model, in which an endowment of $10 million would have ensured the continuity of the center. Given the concerns for turf and the ever-shifting priorities of the foundation world, and given the short attention span of government agencies, that level of support has to be put together up front when a window of opportunity, created by some fortuitous collection of events, presents itself. Perhaps the center ought not have been launched without the endowment, but then the body of experience gained by the center's successes and failures would not be available to help guide future efforts to place rural development issues on the national agenda in useful, timely fashion.

NINE

A Final Word
Or More

We have presented definitions, concepts, lessons we think we learned, recommendations we hope will be funded, and our view of the center's closing. That's a lot of territory covered, which suggests a summary might be useful if not in order.

The goal of rural development is the same as the goal of any progressive society: to decrease dependency and increase opportunities, keeping in mind the needs of future generations and the demands of nature. Rural development focuses on issues affecting that goal in smaller communities. However, we create unnecessary barriers and unproductive competition by arbitrarily dividing the nation in two—metropolitan and nonmetropolitan—or even in three—urban, suburban, and rural—parts. The nation is a continuum of different size places ranging from the very small to the very large. For reasons of size, geography, resources, discrimination, and history, communities, regardless of size, are at different stages of development and have different resources (natural, financial, and human) with which to work. Both public and private development policies need to be flexible and supportive rather than rigid and directive to respond to this diversity. Further, development begins with people, is achieved by people, and ends with people. Development policies, then, also should be designed to enable and empower rather than to determine outcomes. A new courthouse creates temporary construction jobs; a new highway that allows products or produce to reach markets may enable a local economy to prosper, but not, of course, unless businesses also have access to capital, land, trained workers, and perhaps technical advice.

Unfortunately, bureaucracies (public, private, and academic) almost by definition are rigid, demanding of short-run and highly visible products (academics excepted), and fragmented by issue, department, program, or discipline. Further, institutional memories are vague at best, and the public sector has the added factor of frequent changes of leadership, with each generation seeking its own short-run, highly visible product.

In fairness to the federal bureaucracy, the fault also lies with Congress, where time horizons range from two to six years. In voting for and demanding results from developmental programs, politicians and the public would do well to remember these words of the late Philip A. Hart, a U.S. senator from Michigan: "It is easier to solve technical problems than social problems. Ten years is enough time to build a spaceship, but it is only a blink of an eye in the history of man's long ascent toward a just and humane society."*

The difficulty for smaller communities is compounded by their size and location. Neither their potentials nor their problems are visible enough to gain national attention. As a result, these problems and potentials tend to be ignored or, if addressed at all, considered as an adjunct to programs designed for larger communities, which

---

* Janey B. Hart, "In the Furor over the Building, Don't Forget the Man," *Washington Post,* 5 November 1982.

have different resources. However, for the individuals involved—the entrepreneur with a good idea but no access to capital, or the poor person without access to a decent paying job, a good education, etc.—the problem is no less for those in smaller than for those in larger communities.

The fact is that our nation will not deliver on its promise of providing opportunities unless it does so in smaller as well as larger communities. And given what we now know about the importance of small businesses creating new jobs* and the potential of new technology to allow if not encourage dispersion of economic activity, and given the increased number of people opting for smaller-scale working and living environments, both the private and public sectors have additional incentives to pay more attention to sound development policies for smaller communities.

It is also a fact that our society will not deliver on its promises to diminish poverty, reduce unemployment, eliminate racism, provide sound housing, improve education, and ensure a healthy environment unless it does so in smaller as well as larger communities. That is true not only because of the extent of rural poverty and attendant conditions, but also because of the many urban problems caused by the migration of rural poor people to cities—a movement still going on despite the well-publicized "reverse migration." Despite how one chooses to interpret the pronouncements and policies of the Reagan administration, those promises are still on the books, and are likely to remain there.

Assuming the pendulums of public opinion and public policy swing back to a more active public sector (but not

---

* David L. Birch of the Massachusetts Institute of Technology's Program on Neigborhood and Regional Change has documented that most new jobs are created be smaller and young businesses, rather than by the Fortune 500.

to the point reached in the 1960s), the challenge facing those understanding the importance of rural development is not only to design effective public and private sector development policies, but also to get those concerns on the national agenda and keep them there. That challenge is being made more difficult because the policies of the Reagan administration are eliminating whatever momentum had been built under the Carter presidency and because the federal government is cutting back on already inadequate data collection efforts. Without data, trends and problems cannot be identified, and policies cannot be designed and promoted successfully.

To help meet that challenge, we recommend a national rural policy organization and program that will

- create a rural development data base through collection of information at the local level and analysis of secondary data and through advocacy to increase data collection and analysis at the federal level;
- use the information to educate private and public sector opinion and decision makers on rural development issues, to form and inform rural development networks and advocates, and to design and promote rural development policies;
- be the catalyst, because of its professionalism and demeanor, for bringing together representatives of the private sector and public agencies to design efficient, effective, coordinated approaches to rural development; and
- provide "the memory," because of the continuing nature of its program and the increasing knowledge and expertise of its core staff, and provide the pressure to encourage continuity across changing presidential administrations and agency administrators.

We believe that an organization with the recommended program and level of funding could carry out these tasks effectively. We believe the recommendations are based on sound interpretations of the lessons we learned through six years with the National Rural Center.

If one would like to dream a moment, we could recommend creation of

- a national center for the study *and* advancement of microdevelopment policies for smaller communities, with an assured annual budget of $1 million (from endowment or program grants);
- a national center for the study and advancement of microdevelopment policies for larger communities, with an assured annual budget of $1 million;
- five such regional centers for both smaller and larger communities (ten in all), each with $750,000 assured annual funding; and/or
- state centers for both smaller and larger communities, with assured annual budgets of $500,000.

While the national organizations ought to be freestanding and independent, the others could be affiliated with institutions, provided they had the independence to protect their credibility as sources of sound data and as conveners. The centers would be independent of each other, but ought to create a network for the transfer of information and analysis and the coordination of advocacy efforts.

The costs of that recommendation comes to a tidy sum, but not beyond the capacity of foundations operating at the national, regional, state, or local level and the businesses and labor organizations that would benefit from the work of the centers. We do not suggest that such an undertaking would ensure attainment of national development goals, but we do suggest that it could provide

94

information, ideas, and energy to help that effort along in major ways.

If we be dreamers, then we dream only that the American dream be equally accessible in all size communities, to the poor as well as the wealthy.

If we are realists, it is because we understand development is a lengthy, difficult process, but it is the only option for a society that would be just, humane, and free of the burden of dependency.

Appendixes

A Profile Of Rural America

Irma Elo

During the past several decades rural* America has been transformed from a place where most rural people obtained their livelihood from agriculture to a place where an increasing number and range of employment opportunities are available to rural and small-town residents. After experiencing three decades of population out-migration, major consolidations in the agricultural sector, and diversification of the economic base, America in the 1970s witnessed a revival of rural population growth, a movement toward stabilization of the agricultural sector, and continued growth of nonagricultural employment opportunities. The rural economy is now integrated, to a much greater degree than ever before, with the national economy. The industrial mix in rural areas is becoming more like that of urban areas.

At the same time, incomes of rural residents have improved, and rural areas in general can no longer be characterized by economic and social disadvantage. Pockets

Irma Elo was director of the center's Data and Capacity Building Program.

---

*"Rural" and "nonmetropolitan" are used interchangeably throughout the text unless otherwise indicated.

of poverty, however, still remain, and rural areas continue to have a disproportionate share of the nation's poor. The following discussion highlights major changes that have taken place in rural America during the past decades. In addition, a short discussion of rural poverty is provided.

Population Change

About 60 million people live in rural America today. The 1970s witnessed a revival of rural population growth. For the first time in recent American history the nonmetropolitan population grew more rapidly (15.7 percent) than the population in metropolitan areas (9.9 percent). In fact, the 1980 Census indicates that approximately 3.5 to 4.0 million more people moved into nonmetropolitan areas than out of them during the 1970s. This is in sharp contrast to the decade of the 1960s when nonmetropolitan America experienced a net out-migration of 2.8 million people. The growth of rural population was not limited to areas that are urban in character or influenced by nearby metropolitan areas, but also occurred in remote areas and the open country.

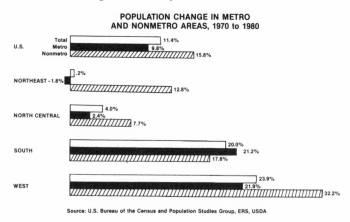

POPULATION CHANGE IN METRO AND NONMETRO AREAS, 1970 to 1980

U.S.
- Total: 11.4%
- Metro: 9.8%
- Nonmetro: 15.8%

NORTHEAST
- -1.8%
- .2%
- 12.8%

NORTH CENTRAL
- 4.0%
- 2.4%
- 7.7%

SOUTH
- 20.0%
- 21.2%
- 17.8%

WEST
- 23.9%
- 21.9%
- 32.2%

Source: U.S. Bureau of the Census and Population Studies Group, ERS, USDA

98

Metro to Nonmetro Migration, 1975-80

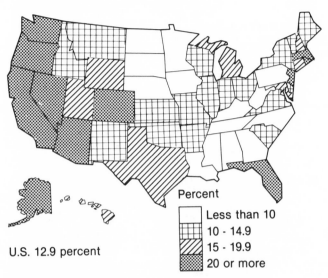

Percent

	Less than 10
	10 - 14.9
	15 - 19.9
	20 or more

U.S. 12.9 percent

1980 data. Percent of 1980 nonmetro population who lived in
metro areas in 1975.
Source: Bureau of the Census.

Notwithstanding the overall revival of rural population
growth, it is important to realize that this growth in the
1970s, just like the decline during the previous decades,
was not uniform across the country. In fact, some four
hundred nonmetropolitan counties continued to experience a population decline in the 1970s. These counties were concentrated in the agricultural areas of the
Great Plains, the Corn Belt, and the southern coastal
plain. In contrast, more than a hundred counties, located
principally in the West, grew by more than 50 percent.

The reasons for the turnabout in rural population decline and growth are varied and are briefly summarized
below. First, after a massive displacement of farm residents, the 1970s witnessed a slowing of changes in the
structure of agriculture. During the previous four decades

Components of Wage and Salary Employment Growth, 1973-82

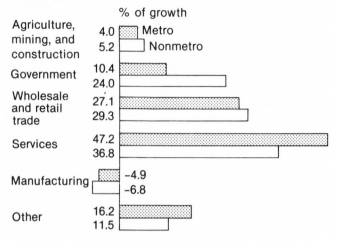

% of growth

	Metro	Nonmetro
Agriculture, mining, and construction	4.0	5.2
Government	10.4	24.0
Wholesale and retail trade	27.1	29.3
Services	47.2	36.8
Manufacturing	-4.9	-6.8
Other	16.2	11.5

Agriculture, mining, and construction includes forestry and fisheries.
Other includes transportation, communications, and public utilities;
finance, insurance and real estate; and private household workers.
Source: Current Population Survey, Bureau of the Census.

some 30 million people had left farms, but the potential for further losses in agriculture had greatly diminished. Second, the diversification of the rural economy with the growth of nonagricultural wage-and-salary jobs has enabled many rural residents, who previously might have been forced to leave in search of jobs, to find employment in rural areas. Finally, the growth of employment opportunities and the modernization of rural life have attracted migrants from urban areas and have enabled many citizens to act out their preferences for a more rural lifestyle.

Economic Structure

Today nonagricultural activities dominate the rural countryside. Although agriculture continues to be an im-

portant source of employment and income in some rural
areas, the majority of rural people depend on nonagricultural jobs for employment. By 1979, only 3.4 percent
of the total U.S. workforce and 8 percent of the work force
in nonmetropolitan America could be classified as agricultural workers, even by the most inclusive definition
(wage and salary, self-employed, and unpaid family).

Since only 8 percent of the nonmetropolitan work force
is employed in agriculture, what industry or industries
have replaced farming as major source(s) of employment
of rural residents? In 1979, manufacturing was the leading
source of employment in nonmetropolitan America, en-
gaging approximately one-fourth of the rural labor force.
Manufacturing was followed by trade and government,
each employing about one-fifth of the labor force, and by

Unemployment Rates for Metro and Nonmetro Areas

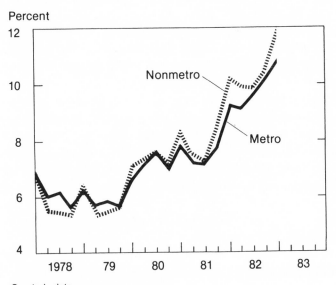

Quarterly data.
Source: Bureau of Labor Statistics.

the service sector, which provided jobs to approximately 15 percent of the rural work force.

While these industry groups provide a larger proportion of employment in rural areas today than during the previous decades, the change has been gradual and not just a recent shift. For example, during the two decades from 1950 to 1970, employment in manufacturing grew by approximately 58 percent, wholesale and retail trade by about 48 percent, and professional and related services by 160 percent even in the most thinly populated areas defined by the Census Bureau as rural (open country and places with fewer than twenty-five hundred people lying outside the urban fringe of metropolitan cities).

The duration and strength of the employment growth in nonmetropolitan America was also evident in the 1970s. Prior to then only manufacturing employment growth in rural areas exceeded the growth in metropolitan America. In contrast, between 1973 and 1982 nonfarm wage-and-salary employment increased more rapidly in every industry group in nonmetropolitan areas than in metropolitan America, except in manufacturing, which declined in both metro and nonmetro areas, and in services, transportation, communications, public utilities, finance, insurance, real estate, and private household workers combined.

The diversification of the rural industrial structure has integrated the rural economy into the national economy, and rural areas are no longer isolated from the forces influencing the national economy. For example, for the first time in a recessionary period since World War II, the nonmetropolitan unemployment rate has consistently exceeded the metropolitan rate. In 1983, the nonmetropolitan annual average unemployment rate was 10.1 percent compared to 9.4 percent in metropolitan areas. And, if one accounts for discouraged and part-time workers, both of whom are a large percentage of the nonmetropolitan labor force, the situation is even worse.

Rural Poverty

During the last three decades the incomes of nonmetropolitan residents have improved relative to those of the residents of metropolitan areas. In 1950, nonmetropolitan median family income was only two-thirds of the metropolitan median, but by 1980 the nonmetropolitan median family income had increased to nearly 80 percent of the comparable metropolitan figure. According to analysts at the Economic Development Division, U.S. Department of Agriculture, the improved income situation was related to increased formal educational, industrial growth and diversification, off-farm employment by farm family members, increased labor force participation by rural women, reduced discrimination against racial minorities, and the growth of government transfer programs.

However, despite these gains rural America continues to be the home for a disproportionate share of the nation's poor: 39 percent of the nation's poor people live in rural areas compared with only 28 percent of the nation's total population. There are groups of people and regions of the country who have not benefited from the "revitalization" of rural areas during the 1970s and the previous decades.

Although the majority of the rural poor are white (since whites are the majority population), rural poverty falls disproportionately on minorities. In 1981, the poverty rate among rural blacks was 42 percent and among rural Hispanics 28 percent, compared with only 14 percent among rural whites. Other groups among the rural residents of whom a disproportionate share live in poverty are the elderly, almost 20 percent of whom have poverty-level incomes, and female-headed households, of whom 40 percent live in poverty. The poverty rate among the nation's farmers also remains high today, although it has drastically declined during the previous decades—from 45 percent in 1959 to 22 percent in 1982.

Rural poverty is not uniformly distributed among regions of the country. Nearly 60 percent of the rural poor live in the South, where 21 percent of the rural population live in poverty. However, rural poverty is not restricted to the South. A number of populous rural counties in the Northeast, for example, have large poverty populations, although they do not have a high incidence of poverty. A further illustration of the persistent poverty found in rural areas is the fact that almost all of the nation's poorest counties are nonmetropolitan and almost all of these counties have been in the lowest income category since 1950.

An often overlooked reality of rural poverty, and one that distinguishes it from urban poverty, is the fact that most of the rural poor work at least part time but are unable to earn above poverty-level incomes. In 1981, almost 70 percent of poor nonmetropolitan households had at least one worker, and almost one-third had two or more members in the work force.

Summary

Rural America cannot be described by generalizations. The issues and problems faced by rural residents and communities are different now than they were ten to twenty years ago. Some areas of the country have to find ways to cope with extremely rapid population growth, while other areas continue to seek ways to capture a share of national employment growth that has passed them by thus far.

104

Much of the progress in rural areas during the past several years was supported by federal assistance. In the 1980s, however, the role of the federal government has diminished, funding for grant and loan programs has been reduced, and responsibilities have shifted to the state and local governments. This has created new challenges for rural institutions, community-based organizations, and others to find ways in which economic and community development activities which began during the past decades can be sustained.

Rural Development: Prospects for Delivery Strategies and Programs In the 1980s

John M. Cornman

The prospects addressed in this paper reflect the view that what is needed is not an urban versus rural development policy, but rather a national development policy with delivery strategies and programs appropriate to urban or rural areas. Such a policy would allow one to muse about prospects for the whole policy as well as the rural elements of that policy. The prospects of both will be affected, if not determined, by international, national, and rural issues, the resolutions of which I am no better prepared to predict than I am to predict the future of strategies and programs themselves. I do not pretend this list of issues is complete or that I have included all the implications of these issues and their ramifications for development in rural areas.

The overriding international concern is peace, or, perhaps more accurately, the degree of peace present over the next decade. A convincing case can be made that the demand for food and need for nonfarm manpower in World War II were major factors in speeding the mechanization of farm operations, reducing the number of farm jobs, and spurring on rural-to-urban migration. Similarly, international confrontations consume resources, and agendas that involve long-term commitments, such as development, do not receive high priority. And, of course, if the confrontation is nuclear, all issues other than survival become moot.

How the United States uses its agricultural capacity and expertise in international affairs will be another major factor in the coming decade. Will we choose to export food to balance our oil deficit or expertise to help nations meet their own needs—or, more accurately, what blend of those choices will we pursue? Equally important will be the method chosen to implement the selected strategies. If, for example, a chosen strategy demands greatly increased production of certain commodities, implementation of the strategy could emphasize research, resources, and/or policies that ignore broader concerns of rural development.

Another international issue which will affect rural development is trade agreements. There is evidence that trade agreements that encourage low-wage industries abroad may succeed at the expense of low-wage industries in domestic rural areas, a traditional way of bringing industries to our rural communities. To offset this, however, the next decade may provide new export opportunities for rural enterprises.

Paramount among international trade issues are those affecting oil, which will affect not only our domestic policies but also our foreign policies and world peace.

National Issues

The list of national issues affecting prospects for rural development begins (or ends, depending at what part of the cycle you begin) with the extent of the nation's commitment to national development goals. Little progress will be made concerning employment, housing, or health problems in rural areas unless there is a commitment to address these issues nationally. Even if such a commitment exists, efforts will continue to be focused on urban areas unless there is broader understanding and acceptance that the nation has a stake in rural development. That stake includes meeting society's responsibility to the poor, 10 million of whom live in rural areas; meeting national goals such as those concerning employment, housing, health, and energy; creating the jobs and markets needed for a viable national economy; and providing job and residential options necessary to the well-being of a free society.

The degree of commitment will be influenced by the degree of inflation and the degree of faith (well placed or not) in the impact of a balanced national budget.

The ability to deliver on the commitment will be affected by the impacts of energy policies (including cost and availability) and new technology on rural development opportunities, and of our willingness and ability to relate macrolevel policies and microlevel programs more effectively in the future.

Will the energy crisis work for or against location of manufacturing and service jobs in rural areas? Will it help or hinder dispersion of food-processing facilities? Will it help or hinder rural residents commuting long distances to jobs? Will new technology encourage dispersion or concentration of jobs and facilities and will it serve smaller scale enterprises and communities as well as larger ones?

108

Will we learn how to transfer the benefits of this technology to meet rural needs? Will we remember the importance of smaller scale enterprises as we debate the reindustrialization of the nation?

Obviously, the migrations caused by all of the above will affect prospects for rural programs in the decade ahead. Will "reverse" migration continue? Who will be moving? How well will we understand what is happening and who is benefiting?

Prospects on the national level also will be influenced by the outcome of presidential and congressional elections. A president committed to rural development can help make up for the lack of an organized constituency, and members of Congress who look beyond special interests can provide needed leadership.

Rural Issues

Certain rural issues are critical to prospects for rural development policies. A better understanding of the diversity of rural areas; an adequate data base; increased capacities of rural people and the institutions that serve them; organizations to influence governments, and public and private sector investment decisions; leaders selected who are committed to development—all will be vital to rural development in the decade coming. . . .

For most of the past two decades efforts to include those omitted from the development process focused on guaranteeing certain rights and securing more equitable distribution of public resources. I think history will show that, as an initial effort, the focus was correct. We will be hard pressed to come up with a rural development act for the South as effective as the 1964 Voting Rights Act. That act dealt with a permanent (I trust) institution: the formal procedure through which citizens select leaders and influence policy. However, many other efforts concentrated on establishing new organizations to deliver services and influence various levels of government. As a result, we have a plethora of citizen-based organizations, coordinating committees, regional commissions, lobby groups, and caucuses concerned with aspects of development. Many of these entities have been established to compete with existing, but nonresponsive, institutions. Whatever the merits of such a strategy, it has yet to deal with two crucial elements—permanency and intellectual base. Forced to live on grants, many of these organizations have had to trim sail or change course in response to the grantsmanship process. Many of the grant makers have had no coherent or consistent development strategy to guide their decisions. Neither has thought been given to providing these organizations with the information required to broaden their perspectives.

What is involved is a fundamental change from a confrontation strategy to a developmental strategy. With a shrinking, or at best static, public grants budget, people interested in development find these organizations severely limited in funds and expertise to make the change. At the same time, many of the permanent institutions that could be important to development in rural areas—the land grant universities, community colleges, planning districts, and traditional citizen groups—have not grown to fill the gaps.

As we recognize that development takes time, patience, and commitment, it is becoming clear that the absence of permanent, responsive institutions with long-term commitments to rural development is a serious barrier.

And finally, to complete this list of factors affecting prospects for rural development in the 1980s is the ability of rural people, with all their diversity, to organize effectively and make themselves heard. Rural people, dispersed, diffuse, and relatively few in numbers, frequently are ill-equipped to compete in the national arena for attention and resources, a cause of many of the barriers discussed above. Given the historic inability of rural people to organize effectively around development issues on a national basis, and given the array of imponderables that could adversely affect rural development, it would be prudent to predict that there are no prospects for any new, major federal rural development programs or delivery strategies in the 1980s.

However, being something of an optimist, I do not believe the picture need be entirely bleak, if rural development advocates are willing to settle for a limited number of important advances and if the research community is willing to address rural development issues in ways useful to policy makers. Given a degree of cooperation between those two worlds, important advances could be made in the quality and quantity of data collected and disseminated; in understanding what is meant by capacity building and how to deliver what, to whom, and when; in learning how to link various development programs for maximum impact; in encouraging the use of small business development as a tool to create new jobs; and perhaps in creating a broader development constituency around these issues.

These advances can be justified in ways consistent with what appears to be the political mood of the decade. Improved information could help program managers make better use of resources under their control. If the data collected involved the private as well as public sectors, the data could be used as a basis for improved private-public sector cooperaion. Further, if encouragement of small businesses turns out to be a useful way to create new jobs, efforts in the area could attract the support of

111

a wide range of interests—starting with small business and full employment constituencies, but extending to constituencies concerned with development in general, civil rights, tax reform, small farms, conservation, and economic concentration.

Finally, I can predict that if progress is made along these limited fronts in the 1980s, then prospects for rural policies in the 1990s will be greatly enhanced, depending of course on war, peace, energy, agriculture. . . .

Excerpted from *American Journal of Agricultural Economics* December 1980):142-145.

The Corporate Interest In Rural America

John M. Cornman
Harrison H. Owen

C orporate interest in rural communities falls into three categories: societal, pragmatic, and visible. Encompassing 25 percent of the nation's population—and growing—these communities represent a large market for an economy in search of customers. Dispersion of facilities and population will help ease urban problems caused by crowding and lack of opportunity while providing strategic benefits for national security. Prudent use of natural resources, most of which are located in these areas, is necessary to sustain a viable national economy over time. And employment growth in these communities can help create the 15 million new jobs needed this decade to meet the demands of a growing population.

From a pragmatic point of view, these communities can offer attractive plant locations because they may be close to raw materials, attractive to key employees and their families, and more receptive to innovative management organization and labor agreements, and because costs associated with congestion and other urban conditions may be reduced. Also, their attractiveness will increase

113

as telecommunications lessen the importance of transportation and the information and cultural disincentives associated with remoteness.

The impacts of corporate involvement, whether through taxes paid or through support for development activities, will be more visible in smaller communities than in large ones. Corporations can assist in every aspect of the development process, from support for appropriate national policies to participation in various regional bodies to activities in localities where the corporation has its facilities.

Limited or outdated infrastructures restrict the potential of rural communities to attract jobs. Research is needed to devise joint local, state, federal, and private-sector approaches to solving this problem. As some corporate executives have observed, national support for education and training programs is required if the country is to have a work force equipped to compete in the economy of the future. Corporations can help ensure this need is met in rural as well as urban areas.

Agriculture, industry, and housing have legitimate but competing claims on land and water in rural areas. Fossil fuels are at once a local and a national resource. How conflicts arising from such claims are resolved will affect the viability of many rural areas as well as the long-term welfare of the nation. Corporations can encourage thoughtful consideration of such issues.

In urban areas, corporations support elements of existing strategies: the arts, higher education, public schools, neighborhood revitalization, job training. Because they are small, rural communities often lack the capability to plan development strategies, identify potential opportunities, and attract resources—particularly capital. In the absence of such strategies, corporations can make mean-

114

ingful contributions in rural areas by providing expertise and technical assistance as well as dollars.

Because of its history of noninvolvement in rural development issues, the corporate sector could begin by

- creating a rural or small-towns focus in its strategic planning, public and community affairs, and corporate giving offices to learn about rural development issues and to identify appropriate opportunities for corporate involvement;
- cooperating with other corporations and appropriate public agencies and interest groups to encourage establishment of private-public sector regional forums on critical resource allocation issues; and
- ensuring that rural concerns are included in its positions on national issues, such as employment training programs, capital formation, and public works financing.

In summary, corporations not only have an important direct and indirect stake in rural development; they can be a powerful force in helping rural areas fulfill their potential.

A Challenge For
Private Foundations

John M. Cornman

For twenty years, the pendulum of public opinion supported increased intervention by the public sector, particularly the federal government, to help correct societal and economic inequities. New programs followed new programs, and most tended to focus on small fragments of the problem: preschool education, job training, business loans, industrial parks, medical care, lunch at schools, etc. Little effort was made to document the total impact of these efforts at the local level or to learn how these programs ought to work together and with the private sector. Instead, what were experimental programs became fixtures, taking on a rigidity born of program regulations and bureaucratic self-interest.

During the same period, many private foundations, seeking to ensure an impact for their dollar, followed suit by focusing as narrowly as possible on a few issues. Replicability was often a goal of their projects but was seldom achieved. Lessons learned from successes and failures often disappeared with the project, and, not unlike federal bureaucracies, foundations were reluctant to relate to efforts of other foundations.

Now, as it inevitably does, the pendulum of public opinion swings in the opposite direction, toward reduced public sector intervention and increased reliance on the private sector. Without information about what has worked, defenders of existing public programs support flawed and successful experiments alike or lament the absence of a new agenda; practitioners scramble for resources without a knowledge base on which to build increased chances for success; and foundations struggle to sort out the greatly increased requests for money.

While those who want to reduce intervention by the public sector may be no more knowledgeable about the impacts of program cuts than supporters of the programs, it is not the responsibility of those opposed to public sector intervention to document and evaluate the experiments of the past twenty years. That should have been done by the architects, operators, and funders of the experiments, and it was not.

More importantly, unless efforts begin now to document trends, impacts, and experiences at the local and substate levels, the lessons of the recent past and of the current approach to public policy will go unrecorded. As a result, those lessons will be lost to future policy makers and practitioners. Those who would govern when the pendulum of opinion reverses its swing will be no better equipped to know where public sector intervention can be efficient and successful than were those who launched the experiments of the 1960s and 1970s.

There will be one important difference, however. The public will not be as patient in accepting experimentation and broad public sector involvement. That means the innovative agenda for the 1980s must be based on a body of experience that both increases the likelihood of success and gives the public reason to believe in that likelihood.

To be useful, a documentation effort must look at issues rather than at programs:

- at job creation and who gets the jobs, not at skill training or industrial park programs by themselves;
- at health status and what affects that status, not at grants for health clinics or housing and water and sewer programs by themselves;
- at efforts to relieve poverty, not at income maintenance, food stamp, or housing programs by themselves; and
- at the ability of communities to identify problems, select priorities, and plan and carry out development strategies, not at narrow planning grants or technical assistance programs by themselves.

There is absolutely no reason to believe that the federal government will fund such an effort, and there is little likelihood that academia will do so on its own accord or could do so with the necessary interdisciplinary and policy-oriented approach.

That leaves private foundations. Not only does the task fall to foundations by default; it is also consistent with their independent mission to examine and evaluate the best of the private and public sectors and to recommend how those sectors can work together better. Further, they could take on this task without changing their current program priorities and, by pooling resources, without a major drain on resources.

That is the challenge for private foundations. By accepting it, foundations could help develop thoughtful agendas based on experience for their on-going programs and for public policy. By refusing it, they, in the terms of one foundation official, would continue to "thrash around."

The National Rural Center: Goals and Objectives

The Board of Directors of the National Rural Center approved the following goals and objectives statement at the Janaury 1979 meeting.

I. Assumptions on Which the National Rural Center Was Organized

A. The term "development" encompasses the many dimensions or conditions that determine the quality of life: access to public services and facilities; economic growth; protection and enhancement of natural and environmental resources; and the capacity of people, communities, and public and private institutions to interact in identifying and attaining these and related goals.

B. Government policies ought to reflect a comprehensive approach to development and ought to work to increase the options people have for a decent life in the kind of community in which they choose to live.

C. To be effective, development policies must respond to the diverse needs of the many different kinds of areas, communities, and neighborhoods where the quality of life is declining or is substandard.

D. Low-income people in rural and urban communities have pressing unmet needs, some of which can be alleviated through more responsive national policies and programs.

E. The success of any urban development strategy depends on avoiding through positive measures a resumption of the vast rural-to-urban migration that left many rural areas depleted and urban places more crowded—a migration that too often meant a move from rural poverty to urban poverty.

F. Existing national policies and programs reflect concern for neither the poverty found in rural areas nor the relationship between a national rural strategy and a successful urban strategy.

G. The primary responsibility for the evolution and implementation of a development strategy lies with rural people themselves, though a number of supporting institutions are required. These institutions include

1. local, state, regional, and national advocacy organizations that can effectively voice rural concerns and solutions;

2. institutions that provide technical and capacity-building assistance to assist rural people, identify, articulate, prioritize, and attain development goals;

3. public and private agencies that supply financial assistance needed to attain goals; and

4. institutions that help develop policy alternatives and encourage the flow of informa-

tion among rural people, the institutions that support them, and policy makers.

H. Because of the limited amount of funds available for public-interest activities, particularly those related to rural concerns, and because one organization cannot respond to all the institutional needs of rural people, the National Rural Center should exist only if it serves one of the institutional needs of rural people and, in doing so, brings unique resources to bear on rural problems.

I. The National Rural Center, although it has a deep concern for the rural poor, can play a unique role because it does not have to be responsive to a specific membership, it is not narrowly focused by geographic or subject area, and it is not tied to the survival of specific institutions or strategies.

II. *Statement of Mission*

The mission of the National Rural Center is to collaborate with other private and public organizations in the development and implementation of national rural policies and programs that will increase the options people—and particularly the rural poor—have for a decent life in rural areas.

III. *National Rural Center Goal*

The goal of the National Rural Center is to gather, develop, analyze, and disseminate information to rural people, the institutions that represent their concerns, and national policy makers in an attempt to make national programs more responsive to the needs of the rural poor. By 1985 the federal government should have in place a process whereby rural people can participate in the development of national strategies that will lead to programs that are appropriate to their needs. Also by 1985 the federal government should have shown considerable progress in alleviating the most serious problems that are now affecting rural America.

The evaluation of the National Rural Center's progress towards its goal must be based on the extent of change within the federal government and an assessment of the center's role in contributing to this change. This will be the basis upon which the president reports annually to the board. The goal is based on the year 1985 so that the board of directors will force itself to review the role of their institution in promoting change during the period 1979–1985. The board will reserve funds for and commission a comprehensive evaluation of the National Rural Center's impact during this period. This evaluation will begin in January 1986 and will be conducted by an advisory panel consisting of elected officials, national policy makers, rural development practitioners, and rural, low-income people. Unless this panel directs otherwise, the center will cease to exist as of June 1987. Assets and resources that should be continued (such as the library) will be distributed according to corporate dissolution plans.

IV. **Strategies for Attaining Goal**

A. *Operational Strategies*

These strategies are based on the active verbs in the first sentence of the National Rural Center's goal statement: gather, develop, analyze, and disseminate.

1. Gather Information

The center will continue to expand its library collection through information networks in the academic sector, public-interest sector, business sector, and government sector. Formal relationships will be established with other specialized libraries with a rural focus. Area specialists will be brought together to assess the state of the literature on any given subject category. Information regarding pending federal legislation will be collected by monitoring the development of policies, programs, and regulations as they are discussed. The center will also encourage other groups both public and private to collect information that is relevant to rural development issues. Through efficient communication links such as toll-free telephone lines and regional offices, the center hopes to obtain firsthand information on rural problems and concerns.

2. Develop Information

Where the center collaborates with other individuals and groups to assess the state of the art within subject area research, it will strive to fill those informational gaps that are identified. This may be accomplished by demonstrating alternative policies and programs and documenting the results. In some cases this task may also involve the evaluation of existing projects or impact assessments of general policies. In cases in which the center does not have the institutional capacity to fill these information gaps, it will recommend to policy makers that resources be provided to other private institutions or government agencies to collect this data.

3. Analyze Information

Based on the analysis of the information that is collected and developed by the center and others, the center staff should be in a position to offer sound policy and program recommendations to national policy makers. These recommendations will be developed in concert with rural development practitioners, through issue conferences and in ad hoc advisory groups. At no time will the center lose track of the fact that development strategies are best designed by those for whose benefit they exist.

4. Disseminate Information

The center has identified three primary client groups for whom its information is intended:

a. *Rural development practitioners,* including rural service institutions, elected officials, and concerned rural citizens. To these groups the center will provide within the limitations of its institutional capacity information on available resources for their local development efforts. In most cases the center will attempt to synthesize this information into publication form for general distribution. In some cases, however, the center will respond in a more personalized manner through letters and toll-free telephone contact. A limited number of this client group may also receive subject newsletters and issue papers regarding pending national legislation that may affect their development efforts.

b. *National policy makers,* including federal officials, members of Congress, foundation and private sector executives, public-interest groups, and lobbyists. This client group will not only receive subject newsletters and issue papers, but, more importantly, they will receive the center's well-documented policy alternative recommendations. It is anticipated that this distribution will have a catalytic effect in bringing about changes within national rural development policies. Whenever possible, the president of the center will make presentations to interested groups and congressional hearings regarding these policy alternatives.

c. *The general public.* This client group will receive information regarding the general conditions and realities of rural America. This will be disseminated through newspapers, wire services, and national magazines.

B. *Institutional Strategies*

To build the capacity it needs to pursue its mission effectively, the National Rural Center will

1. develop a professional core staff that believes in the center's purpose and goals and has skills and experience that encompasses the center's comprehensive approach to development and a national rural strategy;

2. develop a library of information that encompasses the present state of the art of rural development knowledge and resources, and organize this information for responsive retrieval;

3. develop direct lines of communication to rural people and the institutions support-

ing them through the maintenance of mailing lists, toll-free telephones, and regional offices; and

4.   develop internal management and evaluation systems to ensure the center's progress toward its goals.

V.   *Planning Process*

A.   *Priority Selection*

In selecting program areas to be developed, the board and management will consider in general:

1.   the importance of the subject area in improving the quality of life for rural people, particularly the rural poor;

2.   the real or potential impact that national policies or programs in the subject area have or could have on the quality of life for rural people;

3.   the degree and effectiveness of efforts of other organizations involved in the area, and the ability of the center to bring needed and additional resources to the subject area;

4.   the potential opportunity for the center to effect policies and programs within a two- to five-year period; and

5.   the extent of activity in any given subject area, determined by the amount of funding available. Also, at the discretion of management and with concurrence of the board or a subcommittee of the board, the

center may choose to respond to "targets of opportunity" that are important to its overall goal and mission.

B. *Program Development*

In selected subject areas, the center will seek to secure in-house expertise and develop and carry out a public policy research and information gathering program. The end products of a program are to be policy recommendations and implementation efforts, a research agenda for others to pursue, and examples of the kinds of information rural people need. In addition, recommendations will be made so that this kind of information can be provided through permanent institutions and on a continuing basis.

To develop a program, the staff will

1. carry out a review of national policies to determine primarily what the federal government is doing, should be doing, should stop doing, or should do better;
2. develop a selected bibliography of data sources for use in building library resources and assisting others interested in the subject area;
3. prepare a list of organizations with whom the center should collaborate in securing policy changes;
4. develop a research strategy;
5. identify information needs; and
6. establish evaluation criteria for program areas, policy projects, and information activities.

Publications
Of the National
Rural Center

I. Data and Capacity Building

Directory of Rural Organizations
Directory of State Title V Rural Development
    Programs
The Essential Process, A policy statement on
    the Title V Program of the 1972 Rural
    Development Act
An Approach to Rural Needs Assessment
Private Funding for Rural Programs, A direc-
    tory of foundations and others.
Resource Guide for Rural Development
Rural Development and the Land Grant
    University
Rural Poverty
Rural Poverty and Transfer Payments

II. Economic and Community Development

Balanced Growth, A review of regional and devel-
    opment policies of European governments
Options in Regional Incentive Policy
Regional Incentives in Canada

Regional Incentives in Britain
Evaluation of Regional Economic Policies
Regional Incentives in France
Regional Incentives in Italy
*Executive Summary on Balanced Regional
    Growth Conference*
Regional Incentives in Germany
Regional Growth Policies in the United States
*Restrictive Regional Policies in the European
    Community*
*Bibliography of Small Farms Research, 1970 to
    1977*
A Review of Selected Small Farms Projects
*Development Finance: A Primer for Policy
    makers,* A three-part report on the potential
    and design of public development finance
    policies
Energy and Small Farms, A review of
    literature and suggestions for further
    research
*The Influence of Federal Policy on Urban
    Economies*
Marketing and the Small Farm
*Report on National Rural Community Facilities
    Assessment Conference*
Off-Farm Earnings and Small Farms
*Public Agriculture—Food Policies and Small
    Farms*
*The Rural Income Maintenance Experiment,
    Welfare Reform and Small Farms*
Southern Rural and Agricultural Development
*Farm and Non-Farm Uses of Farm Family
    Resources*
*Structure of Agriculture and Small Farms In-
    formation Needs*

Toward a Small Farms Policy
The U.S. Tax Systems and the Structure of
  American Agriculture
Directory of Small Farms Technical Assistance
  Resources
A Research Agenda for Small Farms
Small Farms Policy on Credit and Taxes
Development Incentives to Induce Efficiencies in
  Capital Markets
On the Need for a National Development Bank
Production Efficiency, Technology and Small
  Farms
A White House Rural Initiative in Transition:
  The Impact of Large-Scale Construction
  Projects on Rural Economic Development
South Texas Rural Employment and Develop-
  ment Project
Increasing Efficiencies in Federal Water and
  Wastewater Programs
An Assessment of Small Cities Block Grants
  Policy
Equal Employment Programs in the Sunbelt
Rural Economic Development in the United
  States
The Rise of the Factory in Rural America:
  Changes in Manufacturing Employment in
  Nonmetropolitan Areas

III. Education

Revitalizing Rural Education
Federal Education Programs in Rural Areas
Between a Rock and a Hard Place: A Planning
  Report on Rural Education in America
Data Report on Small Rural Schools

IV. Health

Medicaid in Rural Texas Areas
Medicaid Reimbursement for Community Health Centers
Research Agenda on Nurse Practitioners/Physician Assistants
Policy Issues in Practice Settings for Nurse Practitioners/Physician Assistants
Research Issues Related to Third-Party Reimbursement for NPs/PAs
Third-Party Payment for New Health Providers
Federal Policy and NPs/PAs
Federal Policy and Support of NPs/PAs Training Programs
Report and Recommendations of Southern Rural Health Conference
A Directory of State Rural Health Offices
Health Care in Underserved Rural Areas
Assessment of 1981 Budget Cuts on Rural Health Programs

V. Human Services

Human Resource Development
Issues Affecting Local and Minority Employment on the Tennessee-Tombigbee Waterway, A series of nine papers.
CETA as a Strategy for Rural Development
Rural Jobs From Rural Public Works, A three-part report on research, policy implications, and a manual for local organizations
The Rural Stake in Public Assistance
Federal Youth Programs in Rural Areas, a research report and a policy statement

VI. Miscellaneous

Rural Justice, A beginning assessment of the
   justice system in rural areas
*Report on 1980 Budget and Selected Rural
   Programs*
*The President's Energy Initiative and Effects on
   Rural Areas*
Report on Rural Arts Institute
For the Soul and the Pocketbook, A resource
   guide on arts and rural development
*National Energy Policies and Programs: Im-
   plications for Rural Areas of the Nation*
Community Rural Development Newsletter
Rural Transportation Newsletter
Rural Health Newsletter
Rural Information Bibliography Service

NOTE: **Publications of the National Rural
Center are available from the Rural
Development Center, Department of
Behavioral Science Research, Carnegie
Hall, Tuskegee Institute, Tuskegee In-
stitute, Alabama 36084.**

Index

Index

and federal policy, 62-63. *See also* Future national rural center, goals of; National Rural Center, goals of

Department of Agriculture, 45: Cooperative State Extension Service (CSES), 81

Department of Labor: failure to fund National Rural Center, 81; Office of Research, 23

E

Economic development, definition of, 11

Edna McConnell Clark Foundation, 1: decision against grant to the National Rural Center, 8, 9, 88; grant announced, 7

Environmental Protection Agency, 42

Expanded Food and Nutrition Education Program, 35

F

Family Farm Coalition, 50

Farmers Home Administration, 42

The Ford Foundation, 1

Federation of Southern Cooperatives, 24

Foundations, 44: and rural America, 76-77; rural development policies of, 116-117, and documentation efforts, 118

Fund-raising, 7: competition, 61; and a future national rural center, 63

Future national rural center, proposals for, 63-64, 77-78: administration of, 70; budget suggestions for, 71-75; and farming, 77; functions development im-

pact assessment project of, 64-65; rural minorities project of, 65-66; rural policy seminars and scholars project of, 66; rural reference service of, 69-70; state briefings of, 68; status of rural America project of, 67-68

G

Goals. *See* National Rural Center, goals of; Future national rural center, goals of

Growth, in rural America, 4-5

H

Hart, Senator Philip A. (D-Mich), 91

Health care, 15: and National Rural Center programs, 39-40. *See also* Networking, of National Rural Center

Housing Assistance Council, 50

I

Information dissemination: rural development library, 30-31; Rural Information Bibliographic Service (RIBS), 31

J

Johnson, President Lyndon B., 1

K

Kentucky Mountain Housing Development Corporation, 36

Kettler, Roman, 35-36
Kincaid, Barbara K., (chief information officer), 7

L

LSU Cooperative Extention Service, 36

M

Marshall, Dr. Ray, 22-23
Martin, Kenneth M., 77
Military Highway Water Supply Corporation, 37
Minorities. *See* Rural America, population of; Poverty, rural, and minorities; Tennessee-Tombigbee Waterway, and minorities
Minorities People's Council of the Tennessee-Tombigbee Waterway, 24

N

National Rural Center, close of, 79, 86-89: and corporate strategy, 82-83; and federal strategy, 81-82; and foundations, 87-88; and foundation strategy, 84-85; and fund-raising strategy, 80-81; and income generating strategy, 83-84
Networking, of National Rural Center, 28-30
Newsweek Magazine, 43
Nonprofit national policy and information groups, organization of: board of directors of, 59-60; core program of, 54, 55, 63; employment policies of,

53-56, 63; federal financing of, 54-55; income generation of, 56-57; interdisciplinary approach in, 52-53; mission, definition of, 57-58; regional offices of, 58-59
Northeast South Dakota Community Action Program, 35
Nuclear Confrontation, 107

O

Office of Technical Assistance, Economic Development Administration (EDA), 81-82
Owen, Harrison H., 113

P

The People Left Behind, 1
Policy, affecting rural America, 12, 15: and small farms, 16
Policy-making process 12-13: lessons learned about, 41
Policy research, definition of, 12
Poverty, rural, 1, 3: and decision makers, 41-43; and economic improvement, 101; and minorities, 4, 103; and the South, 14, 102; and welfare reforms, 26. *See Also The Rural Stake in Public Assistance*
Professional Reference Service, 83
Publications. *See* National Rural Center, publications; Networking
Public education, and the National Rural Center, 32-33, 38: methodology 33-34. *See also The Winthrop Rockefeller Awards for Distinguished Rural Service*

R

Ramirez, Arturo V., 37
Reagan administration, President Ronald, 92: budget cuts for rural data gathering, 46; election of, 24, 26; ends Carter administration's rural initiative, 26; and National Rural Center's close, 82, 86; and rural development, 42-43
Research and demonstration project. *See* Tennessee-Tombigbee Waterway
Reverse migration, 92, 109
Robb, Charles S., 34
Rockefeller Brother Fund, 1
Rockefeller, Winthrop, 37. *See also* Winthrop Rockefeller Awards for Distinguished Rural Service, the; Winthrop Rockefeller Charitable Trust
Rural, definition of, 2, 5, 9-10
Rural America, 1, 104-105; changes in, 1, 61, 97; economy of, 4, 61-62, 100-103; lack of corporate interest in, 45; and the media, 43-45; and welfare reforms, 26-28
Rural America (organization), 50
Rural America in Passage: Statistics for Policy, 48
A Rural Banking Facility, 40
Rural Clinics Act, 39
Rural Coalition, 50
Rural development, 43-46: and academia, 45; and decision makers, 41-43; definition of, 10-11; and farming, 104-105; and foundations, 44-45; goals of, 90-91; and international issues, 104; and national issues, 105-107; policy devised for, 14-15; problems of, 91-93; prospects for improvement of, 111-112; and rural issues, 109-111
Rural Development Policy Act of 1980, 42
"Rural Development: Prospect for Delivery Strategies and Programs," 106
Rural Health Newsletter, 83
Rural Information Bibliographic Service (RIBS). *See* Information dissemination
Rural Policy Act of 1980, 62
Rural populace, difficulty in organizing, 49-53, 110-111. *See also* Policy, affecting rural America
"Rural renaissance," 2
Rural seminars and scholars program, 84
Rural Sociological Society, 45
The Rural Stake in Public Assistance, 27, 28, 39

S

Senior Staff Associates, Small Town Emphasis Program (Harrisburg, PA), 77
Shafer, Raymond Philip (governor of Pennsylvania), 37
South East Alabama Self-Help Association, Inc., 36
South, rural. *See also* Rural America; Rural poverty
Southern Rural Health Care Conference, 29-30

T

Task Force on Southern Rural Development, 1, 8, 22
Tennessee-Tombigbee Waterway (Ten-Tom Waterway), 22, 38:

and area development, 25-26; funding for, 24; and minorities, 22, 24; and National Rural Center, 23-24; results of, 24-25; and rural employment outreach models, 23, 26
Tuskegee Institute, 32, 56

U

Unemployment. *See* Rural America, economy of
U.S. Corp of Engineers, and the Tennessee-Tombigbee Waterway, 22, 24, 25
U.S. executive branch, rural policies of, 48: fragmentation of, 48-49. *See also* National Rural Center, federal strategy; National Rural Center, closing of

W

Washington, D.C., 63-64
The Washington Post, 44
Winthrop Rockefeller Awards for Distinguished Rural Service, 34-37; factors for success, 37-38
Winthrop Rockefeller Charitable Trust, 80, 85; grant to National Rural Center, 8

Y

Yost, M. Dwayne, 36

JOHN N. CORNMAN was the chief executive officer for the National Rural Center from its founding in 1975 through its closing in 1982, first as executive director, then as president. Earlier, from 1969 to 1975, he was special assistant and director of communications for the late U.S. Senator Philip A. Hart of Michigan. Before coming to Washington as a Congressional fellow in 1964, he was city editor of the *Daily Local News* in West Chester, Pennsylvania, for which he still writes a regular column on national affairs. Since 1983 Mr. Cornman has been the executive director of the Gerontological Society of America in Washington. A native of Philadelphia, he received his B.A. degree in English from Dartmouth College in 1955.

BARBARA K. KINCAID was born in Charleston, West Virginia, but grew up in St. Louis, Michigan, a rural community about fifty miles north of Lansing. She was graduated from Michigan State University in 1968 and shortly thereafter came to Washington as a staff assistant to Senator Philip Hart. In 1977 she joined Mr. Cornman at the National Rural Center as its information director. She is now director of public information at USO World Headquarters in Washington.